— JAMIE THOM —

TEACHER RESILIENCE

MANAGING STRESS AND ANXIETY
TO THRIVE IN THE CLASSROOM

JOHN CATT

First published 2020

by John Catt Educational Ltd,
15 Riduna Park, Melton,
Woodbridge, Suffolk IP12 1QT

Tel: +44 (0) 1394 389850
Email: enquiries@johncatt.com
Website: www.johncatt.com

ISBN: 978 1 913622 22 0

Set and designed by John Catt Educational Limited

REVIEWS

At the opening anecdote, this book had me hooked. I could relate to the moment it described so much; in fact, I am convinced that every other teacher in the country would also feel this connection. That is why this book is so important. As usual, Jamie Thom makes a brilliant point: teachers are not specifically trained in resilience and practical strategies for resilience.

Teacher Resilience delivers exactly what it promises. Its exploration of teacher mental health and wellbeing presents readers with anxiety-inducing scenarios they may face, followed by the wisdom of its inspirational author, who gives practical advice on how teachers can build their resilience, evidenced by educational research. I felt calmer and better equipped to handle my next challenge after reading it. This book is not just important – it is vital in tackling the teacher retention crisis, particularly during these challenging times in education. Every SLT should buy it for their staff. A must-read.

Haili Hughes, author of *Preserving Positivity*

Much is written about wellbeing and resilience at an organisational level. Much is also written at the individual self-help level. In this book, Jamie manages to interweave the big picture of the education sector, the organisational level of the school, and the individual's responsibilities for developing wellbeing and resilience. Drawing on sources as diverse as ancient and modern history, pop culture, academic research and his own and others' practice, Jamie has written a one-stop-shop book for all things sensible, witty, insightful and, most importantly, useful about building resilience in schools.

For any teacher who has faced the lesson from hell and any school leader wishing to shine a light on the importance of developing resilience in their organisation, this book acts as a reminder of the importance of our work as educators and demonstrates how we can best serve our communities and ourselves through a pragmatic approach to developing resilience. Jamie's warmth and wisdom shines from every page. I challenge any educator not to find this book useful and uplifting in equal measure.

Emma Turner, author of
Be More Toddler: a leadership education from our little learners

Teacher Resilience is a marvellous overview of the constituent elements of wellbeing. It focuses on what it takes to flourish, not just survive, in teaching. Jamie offers helpful ways of reframing the negative consequences that arise from the demands of work, underpinned by well-established research. By including an honest account of his own experiences, Jamie helps us to take sensible steps to truly thrive.

Mary Myatt, author of *Back on Track: fewer things, greater depth*

Teacher Resilience has changed my outlook on the concept of wellbeing. We focus our attention, more often than not, on the negatives facing the teaching profession. What Jamie does so succinctly is address the real issues facing teachers, not just narrate them. The calm and subtle tone of the book emphasises that resilience is something that can be built over time. Jamie moves away from cliched ideas about stress and conceptualises the reality of teaching through anecdotal sections that relate to personal experiences. Not only is *Teacher Resilience* exceptionally strong with regard to the suggested approaches to dealing with resilience, but it is also warm and inviting, instantly calming and completely relatable.

Adam Riches, author of *Teach Smarter: efficient
and effective strategies for early career teachers*

In this book, Jamie provides a thoughtful exploration of what we mean when we talk about resilience, who might have it and what we can gain by having it. He also examines what specific barriers might exist for those in education and how we can be empowered, and empower others, to become more resilient. The anecdotes Jamie has included from his fellow teachers are powerful indicators that we are not alone when we feel vulnerable in our work, and he looks at how the complexities of teaching and the pressures placed on the profession can lead to some of us feeling less resilient than others. He also draws on research as he considers elements such as the benefits of sleep to our wellbeing.

Importantly, Jamie provides practical ways to reflect upon ways of thinking, leading the reader consider their own path forward and how to ensure they are better equipped to deal with the issues they may be facing, especially in the circumstances 2020 has presented. He includes information on how to deal with conflict, the benefits of meditation and mindfulness (but also the limitations), how exercise can help and approaches to situations such as interviews or observations.

Ringing out from every page is Jamie's desire to support those in the teaching profession. Ideas of kindness, both to others and ourselves, compassion and empathy – alongside simple strategies to shift your practices and thinking – are presented clearly and persuasively. The Serene Summary at the end of each chapter leaves you with something to ponder as you head off to your next challenge.

Zoe Enser, co-author of *Fiorella and Mayer's Generative Learning in Action*

CONTENTS

Continued ☛

Part IV: In the classroom

Part V: Leadership

FOREWORD

Teacher Resilience is a book that stands apart from the rest, for its careful, quiet compassion for our profession. It offers a platform for discussions that perhaps, in some schools, we have been reluctant to have. In a place and at a time when it is not always acceptable to admit that professional expectation and endurance are challenging, teacher resilience has become something of an assumption. There is a misperception that if teaching is tough, you're teaching right. However, as many of us know all too well, that narrative is highly problematic: "It is the nature of the job" is not a sentence that aims to nurture, protect and sustain our profession. It is inexcusable in its tone and does not offer the perspective that is so desperately required.

Jamie Thom provides a refreshing alternative to the "test of endurance" with an intricate examination of how we achieve *eudaimonia* (page 16), flourishing in the safety of a set of strategies that enable us to fulfil our potential. This book looks at the hidden corners of teaching that are seldom addressed. It seeks to make it acceptable to shine a light upon those less comfortable aspects, before providing a steady hand to help us wrangle with them. In a quest for a true sense of teacher purpose, Jamie highlights the impact of martyrdom in schools, outlining teacher autonomy as vital to building the resilience that empowers us to face the challenges unique to our profession.

The first section of the book identifies why resilience is key to developing our sense of endurance in times of challenge. We are presented with a multitude of ways to contribute to high resilience in our schools. Intrinsic motivation and a strong core purpose are fundamental to ensuring that teachers stay in the job. And as we develop a sense of self-awareness in how we approach difficult situations and times when our resilience is under attack, this newfound consciousness strengthens our ability to tackle such issues head-on. In his book *Drive*, Daniel Pink says we should move away from viewing moments of achievement as our most significant accomplishments, and instead focus upon an "ethic for living".[1] Jamie provides us with a solid rationale for how resilience enables us to fall in love with the journey of self-development.

As teachers, our "inclination towards pessimism" can be a monumental stumbling block when it comes to fighting moments of fragility within the classroom. And, as Jamie points out, we are our own worst enemies. Looking to

---

1   Pink, DH. (2009) *Drive: the surprising truth about what motivates us*, Riverhead Books

the "staffroom snipers" for words of wisdom, we fall into self-deprecatory traps that feed our insecurities and create barriers. To truly develop, teachers must be enabled to learn from mistakes and "not berate ourselves for them". With an astute focus on tools such as mindfulness and placing relationships above all else, Jamie guides us through the necessary discomfort of learning to become comfortable with imperfection.

For teachers reviewing their professional identity, Jamie provides a roadmap for prioritising physical and mental health in order to build a resilient outlook. He warns against the depiction of the "heroic" teacher and we can nod with recognition as he describes the early-bird markers, in danger of burnout without boundaries or breathers, who refuse to leave school before sundown. The end of digital addiction and a focus on restorative sleep and self-regulation are presented as fundamental ways to protect teachers from being seduced by the next shiny idea. This book also takes us back to the satisfying simplicity of collaboration in schools. It provides an outline for building upon the practice of others in order to take us far away from the "culture of fear" that is rooted in toxic schools, and back to the reasons why we came to teaching in the first place.

The classroom is where our resilience can come most under fire, but this book provides a clear and concise approach to planning for longevity. From tackling anxiety about that difficult class to ensuring that our resourcing and feedback do not act as a hindrance or thief of precious time, we take a careful look at the relationship between what we do and how it impacts us as practitioners. The reader is provided with tools to make conversations with students and parents meaningful and purposeful, so that they reinforce a sense of accomplishment and eradicate doubt about our capability to teach. Reframing classroom strategy as an instrument to aid both student and teacher, Jamie enables us to understand the explicit connection between meaningful work and fulfilment.

Leaders may have all the ingredients for allowing teachers to flourish, but it requires careful consideration to understand what this looks like on a day-to-day basis. Jamie presents leaders with the essential pragmatism to ensure that such strategies are possible. In what can only be described as an uplifting call to arms, he offers the tools that leaders need to future-proof their staff body, liberating us all from catch-out cultures and moving towards an ethos where everyone feels heard, understood and involved in the school community. As Stephen Ramsbottom says in chapter 24, staff wellbeing "is not a box to be ticked but a culture to be developed and lived".

Above all, this book takes a people-centred approach to the most problematic issues faced by teachers, placing compassion and care at the heart of every layer of school culture. Jamie provides a refreshing and invigorating set of proposals that reassure me that the future of teaching is utterly autonomous. This is a guide that promises to make resilience a reality for every single teacher who needs it and leaves the profession completely empowered at just the right moment.

Kat Howard

Assistant principal and author of *Stop Talking About Wellbeing*

To Mum and Dad, two wonderful and compassionate teachers who embody all the diverse qualities of true resilience. I hope both your retirements are full of happiness and joy

INTRODUCTION

Anxious anecdote

"Bryanna, can I have some more focus from you, please?" David was aware of the note of pleading in his voice. There was certainly none of the "assertive calm" that the tutors on his training year had claimed was the key to managing "classroom climate".

With impeccable timing, Bryanna delivered a spectacular eye roll – one that was very clear to the rest of the class. The disdain was even more evident in her sarcastic reply: "I don't know. Can you?"

Predictably, the class broke into exaggerated hoots of laughter. All eyes were on David: how would he react?

Twenty minutes later, the class had left and David's forehead was plastered to his desk. "They all hate me," he thought. "I'm useless. What's the point? They are never going to learn anything. I can't go on."

We have all been there. Forever ingrained in our memories are our own versions of the head-on-the-desk moment. We have all felt the burning shame; the sense that we are utterly inadequate and teaching is just too challenging to persevere with. We have all met our own versions of Bryanna.

Painfully, and often reluctantly, most of us eventually lift our heads off the desk. Then, in an emotional transition that could win an Oscar, we smile and welcome the next group of young people into our rooms. Our self-esteem has taken another hammer blow, but we pick ourselves up, take a deep breath and keep going.

It is no exaggeration to suggest that this capacity to rise, both physically and metaphorically, is fairly unique to the teaching profession. If ever there was a job that required superhuman physical, psychological and emotional reserves, it is teaching. This test of endurance, which challenges us on so many fronts, is a significant factor in why retention rates in teaching can appear so depressing. It also goes some way towards explaining why the rate of teachers leaving the profession in the first five years is so high, at somewhere between a third and half in the UK over the past 10 years.

Teacher burnout is common. As we all know, the demands placed on teachers' mental health are significant. We are all too conscious of how unpredictable a day in teaching can be and the emotional impact of this on individuals. In this book, I will argue that it is the elusive and under-explored quality of resilience that is the secret ingredient all teachers need in order to thrive in our profession. To teach effectively and to sustain a long career in education, resilience is required in abundance. Why, then, is resilience not discussed more often in conversations about teaching?

Teacher stress

I have taught for 12 years, in schools from London to Newcastle to Edinburgh. I have sat in countless CPD sessions. I have invested considerable time in academic educational research to doctorate level, and in reading far too many books on education. Yet I have never had any explicit training on resilience, nor have I found myself equipped with practical strategies to ensure I can take ownership of my emotions in the classroom.

Instead of exploring teacher resilience, the conversation is fixed on the headline topics of teacher stress and teacher burnout. Discussions about wellbeing are skewed towards what it is not, rather than how to achieve it. Long hours, excessive accountability and poor retention figures are shouted from the rooftops, but this has the effect of putting more teachers off the profession, rather than illuminating ways in which we can make it more sustainable on an individual level.

It is an interesting snapshot of a culture that often swings towards the negative, rather than being solution-focused. A quick search on the most obvious indicator of societal interest, Google, reveals even further the disparity between explorations of teacher stress and teacher resilience. Googling the term "teacher stress" generates a rather terrifying 346,000,000 results. "Teacher resilience", on the other hand, turns up 50,500,000 results. On its own, this seems a sizeable number, but even with my lack of mathematical skill I can see just how big the disparity is (295,500,000 – I googled it).

Research has shown that some school environments are doing much better than others when it comes to fostering resilience in their staff and in the young people they teach. There is, therefore, a moral imperative for us to look at best practice and examine this vital question in depth: how can we build resilience in the teacher workforce?

The definition

We should start at the beginning: what exactly is this elusive quality of resilience? A journey through the etymology of "resilience" provides some justification for the suggestion that it should be more prominent in discussions of teacher wellbeing. The word stems from the Latin *resiliens*, present participle of *resilire*, meaning "to rebound, recoil". The root re- means "back" and *salire* means "to jump".[2]

In the 1640s, resilient was used to describe "springing back". The meaning "elasticity" dates from 1824, while the use of resiliency to describe "power of recovery" dates from 1857. Springing back, being elastic, recovery: these all strike me as fairly important in the hierarchy of teacher skills. Today, "resilience" is often used in terms of adapting in the face of adversity – bouncing back, persevering and coping. It relates to how we adapt to stressful situations and experiences in order to protect ourselves from further stress.

The qualities

Some lucky individuals appear to glide through their work with young people; they are visions of tranquillity who smile and embrace all challenges. Others (me) might give the impression of serenity, but beneath the calm surface there is not only a furious cacophony of paddling, but also a Metallica-style heavy metal concert of fear, worry and concern.

People who are resilient do, of course, experience feelings of stress and anxiety, but they are not governed by them. Instead, they have at their core the following five qualities:

1. **Perspective**. For those who are resilient, difficulties are not something to be afraid of, nor do they paralyse and lead to inertia. Instead, there is a healthy level of detachment and a belief that challenges allow opportunities for growth.
2. **Commitment**. A resilient outlook means you are committed to the goals and projects that you want to see through; resilience bestows the qualities of perseverance and determination. What young people in schools need, now more than ever, is a sense that we are with them for the long haul – that we will value and cherish them for a sustained period of time. Such a commitment is the foundation of positive relationships in schools.
3. **Control**. People who rate themselves high in resilience tend to focus their energies on the things over which they have control – this is essential in education, where there are so many factors that we cannot control. This kind of mindset is crucial in developing self-efficacy and confidence. It comes with a recognition that the past cannot be changed, but the future is yet to be written.

---

2   www.etymonline.com

4. **Optimism**. Higher levels of resilience help to work against feelings of pessimism, which can be overwhelming. A healthy optimism can create buoyant and positive teachers – teachers that young people want to spend time with and learn from.
5. **Compassion**. Resilience enables you to step outside the internal narrative and consider how other people might be feeling. Building positive relationships and helping others are key to thriving in any environment.

Resilience is not a fixed quality set in stone from a tender age. Rather, research has shown that it can be developed over time – an encouraging piece of information for those of us who sometimes find life in the classroom difficult. In this book, we will examine how we can learn the skills necessary for a resilient mindset, the actions we can take to foster resilience, and how a resilient practitioner might approach the many challenges that we face in the classroom. From parental engagement to differentiation, no pressure point for teacher stress and anxiety will go unexplored.

The wellbeing debate

In schools, "wellbeing" has become an almost hackneyed term, and in many ways it has lost its power. You can see the scepticism that arises in staff when "wellbeing training" takes place. We have all had to sit through wellbeing activities or days that are, at best, a distraction that is of little use and, at worst, a superficial oversimplification.

Rather than achieving "wellbeing", the aim of this book is to help teachers find *eudaimonia*, a delightful Greek term that expresses the capacity for human flourishing. To flourish is a far more optimistic aim: to be in a position to teach and, indeed, learn as well as possible.

Taking ownership

A conversation about what we can do at an individual level to enable this flourishing is vital to make teaching a more sustainable and optimistic profession. Yes, systemic changes are necessary, and I will explore and argue for these. But, fundamentally, the aim of this book is to empower individual teachers who are trying to work out how best to function in schools.

We are, after all, active participants in managing our own health and wellbeing. To leave it down to organisational directives robs us of autonomy over our lives. Rather than accepting things as they are, we need to build the confidence to push back and say no, thus establishing boundaries for ourselves. This is a significant part of developing healthy and robust mindsets in schools. This is resilience in action.

Exploration of mental health and wellbeing is deeply personal and individual. This book is designed to support that exploration – to suggest healthy ways to cope with feelings of stress and the challenges of our profession. It is written with longevity in mind. Trying to attempt all the exercises and suggestions at once will only create more anxiety and stress. Instead, experimenting with the strategies over time will gradually help to build the resilience we all need to thrive in our classrooms.

Resilience in 2020

I started writing this book in January 2020, with the simple aim of reflecting on the best ways to manage stress and anxiety in education. I knew that resilience would be a part of that exploration, but instead it went on to form my central argument about how teachers can sustain themselves in this profession and be the best versions of themselves in the classroom.

As the Covid-19 pandemic tested us in ways that I could never have imagined as I first sat down to write, resilience came to seem even more significant. The necessity of being able to adapt, persevere and maintain optimism has been made painfully clear. Our understanding of personal resilience grew immeasurably during our experience of lockdown.

The time spent away from schools, and away from our core purpose, was a huge challenge, but one that offered time for reflection. As a profession, we have seen that we can do things differently in our schools. We now have an opportunity to look carefully at how teaching can be made more attractive; at how we can make sure talented teachers stay in the profession. We all get better with experience, and schools are so much richer for the experience and wisdom that long-serving teachers bring.

As I write, teachers are desperate to return to the classroom and serve out our purpose: to inspire and motivate young people. It is clearer to society just how essential we are and how challenging teaching is. I hope this book makes a modest contribution to a narrative that moves retention and sustainability in our profession forward; that urges teachers to take ownership and push back against toxic environments and ludicrous workplace practices.

Investing in and prioritising the development of our own personal resilience – and the skills that come with it – will build on the courage and conviction we have shown as a profession during the pandemic. Resilience will help us to thrive, reducing the anxieties and stress that can prevent us from supporting young people. It will sustain us in a challenging profession and help us to bring our best to the role that we love.

Serene summary

Resilience is the quality that allows us to be optimistic and positive about our work – and understanding how to develop that resilience is key to flourishing in the teaching profession. An awareness of the many benefits of resilience is an important starting point in seeking to build it in our professional lives.

PART I: THE IMPORTANCE OF RESILIENCE

'I can be changed by what happens to me.
But I refuse to be reduced by it'
Maya Angelou

1. THE CHALLENGES

Anxious anecdote

An envelope dropped through the letterbox. The front of the card featured the remnants of a single burning candle accompanied by the following quotation:
"A good teacher is like a candle – it consumes itself to light the way for others."

I was 24 and had just passed the interview for a place on a PGCE course to train as a teacher. The card offered heartfelt congratulations on the fact that I had "finally" stepped into "the most meaningful, noble and rewarding of all professions".

I did feel the somewhat unnecessary "finally" and the descriptive triplet, which seemed to pass comment on my two years of procrastination since graduating from university. Fair enough: travelling around Australia and managing a running shop might not have been the most "noble" of endeavours, but surely life experience counts for something in a classroom?

The burnt-out stump of the candle on the front of the card, alongside the quotation from Mustafa Kemal Atatürk, left me feeling slightly uneasy. I was now a self-sacrificing candle? I was on a literal mission to burn out? I was no longer even a singular pronoun, merely an "it"?

My unease grew with the arrival of every card and email. Each was accompanied by another "inspirational" quotation about the "magnificent" career choice I had made. A card that presented a quotation from the American poet Robert Frost seemed very clear on what my future profession would entail: "I am not a teacher, but an awakener."

The next card suggested that teaching was going to be very simple: I merely had to be invisible. It featured a Maria Montessori quotation that informed me, "The greatest sign of success for a teacher is to be able to say, 'The children are now working as if I did not exist.'"

Then I found out that I was going to profoundly influence any child in my presence for the rest of their life. Card no. 4 offered a terrifying prediction from the American historian Henry Adams: "A teacher affects eternity; he can never tell where his influence stops."

So, I was to be an awakening candle who didn't exist, but I would affect my poor charges for all eternity? No pressure.

A look back at these cards today is revealing. Their loud declarations and premonitions, and the lack of agreement between them, indicate some of the reasons why teaching can be so stressful. They also provide further insight into why a dialogue about teacher resilience is fundamental to thriving in the classroom.

Martyrdom

One reason why stress is so pervasive in the teaching profession is that we face such unrealistic expectations. The cards that I received reveal how passionately people feel about teaching, and that strength of feeling can lead to teachers feeling immense pressure to have an impact on young people.

Of course, teachers *can* be utterly transformative, changing lives and having a profound influence on others. This idealistic ambition – perhaps fuelled by the experience of being influenced by a teacher oneself – is often the driving force for people joining the teaching profession. It is one of the amazing things about teaching: the notion of making a difference is not a platitude, it is a reality.

Yet, far too often, this initial enthusiasm can become grinding self-sacrifice. There is a mistaken belief that in order to become one of these life-changing teachers, we must put all other needs before our own. But self-sacrifice certainly does not make us more resilient and robust in schools. In fact, such martyrdom leaves us emotionally fragile and much more susceptible to burnout. This is exacerbated by the pressure of accountability, toxic leadership philosophies and even by teachers themselves – those who narrate the hours they spend on resources, displays and preparing their "masterpiece" lessons.

The vision of "heroic" teachers perpetuated by Hollywood – in emotional stories of teachers who have sacrificed all in their desire to better the lives of their students – adds fuel to the fire. In the 2007 film *Freedom Writers*, the singular devotion shown to her students by Erin Gruwell (played by Hilary Swank) puts a strain on her marriage and she gets divorced. The teachers in *Stand and Deliver* (1988) and *The Ron Clark Story* (2006) are both hospitalised owing to overwork. Hardly a testament to teaching as a balanced career.

Such emotive tales feed the perfectionism that can lead to burnout and result in talented teachers, fed up with every hour of their day being lost to over-preparation, leaving the profession. The simple fact of a life in teaching is that there is never a point at which you feel you are on top of things. There is always more you could do and that can make switching off very difficult. Yet we are striving for unattainable goals that can never be reached.

For those of us inclined to anxiety, there is a sense that we are not doing enough, working hard enough or putting our students first. The temptation to compare ourselves to others is hard to resist and can feed self-doubt. This can create a lonely existence: if we see ourselves as the teaching equivalent of the Lone Ranger, then we risk isolation from all around us. Toxic workplaces exacerbate such emotions: instead of seeking to unite staff, they divide them further.

What is good teaching?

Another stress-inducing feature of teaching is that ubiquitous question: what makes a teacher effective in the classroom? The contrasting philosophies presented in the cards I received, along with governmental influence and the nature of inspection regimes, mean that teachers are often unclear about exactly how they should approach lessons and, indeed, how to build relationships with their students. Should lessons be full of collaboration, with the teacher merely a guide on the side, or should there be much more teacher input? Should we be draconian and never smile, or should we go for a softer/warmer approach?

This is a complex area of debate that opens up thousands of burning questions. There are no simple solutions, and that in itself can amplify teacher doubt and anxiety. In *The Wisdom of Practice*, a collection of essays on teaching and learning, the eminent educational professor Lee Shulman illuminates teaching's intrinsic complexity:

> *"After thirty years of doing such work, I have concluded that classroom teaching is perhaps the most complex, most challenging, and most demanding, subtle, nuanced, and frightening activity that our species has ever invented. The only time a physician could possibly encounter a situation of comparable complexity would be in the emergency room of a hospital during or after a natural disaster."*

For some reason, nobody has yet thought of emblazoning that on a card for new teachers.

Such subjectivity about what good teaching looks like can be challenging for those of us who are prone to anxiety. Everyone seems to have an opinion and that can lead to a lack of clarity. Should research be at the forefront of what we do in the classroom? Should we rely on intuition and our understanding of the young people in front of us? What about that CPD facilitator who told us that "fun" had to be at the core of our lessons? What about the social media wars, in which eminent educationalists passionately decree that knowledge has to be at the heart of teaching?

Then there's the fact that teachers are expected to be fully formed by the end of their NQT year. After two years of support and guidance, NQTs can find themselves adrift as they enter their third year of teaching. Without guidance, they are left to face an increase in pressure and the expectation that they deliver excellent exam results right away. "Feedback" on how to improve can often be sparse. Sometimes, it consists of a mere checklist of senior management's current whims. Inevitably, this leads to struggles that can make the development of confidence and a resilient mindset very difficult.

Under pressure

Pressure is a significant factor in teacher burnout. In schools across the UK, the narrative around exam results is often skewed towards the classroom teacher, not the young people taking those exams.

One of the biggest aggravating factors has been the introduction in England of performance-related pay, with teachers only passing through pay thresholds if their students attain good enough exam results. Although pressure and results will always be a part of teaching, this direct correlation with pay serves only to supercharge levels of stress and anxiety that were already high. League tables and performance management systems worsen the problem. Rather than seeing teachers as striving to improve their students' results, the narrative puts teachers in charge of achieving those results.

Of course, standing up in front of 30 pupils has a cocktail of other anxiety-stimulating features. Teaching is a role in which there is nowhere to hide; no escape from the individuals who watch your every move. And among those 30 young people you will find a range of different needs and emotions: there are those who find it hard to engage in learning, those with behavioural problems, those who have difficulties at home that impact on their learning.

We all like to feel as if we are in control – it is what we do to prevent ourselves from experiencing stress – yet young people are capricious and unpredictable, without the ability to yet monitor their own behaviour in the ways we might hope for. Behavioural issues and communication challenges can contribute to feelings of unease among teachers.

A career in resilience

As my teaching career has progressed (along with the grey hairs and wrinkles), my belief in the necessity of resilience has grown.

In my NQT year, I was faced with a hugely challenging Year 11 class of 15 boys and an instruction to get them to pass their GCSE. What I really needed in this situation were the tools of resilience, not my well-honed knowledge of how to construct engaging group tasks. It was a battle of wills – a bruising experience that required me to take a deep breath every lesson and reach for some inner fortitude.

In my late twenties, when I joined the sizeable number of teachers who have burnt out, a search for inner resilience helped me to take some proactive steps. I moved schools and made changes to my professional life that could help me to cope with teaching. Now, when I wake in the early morning with the anxiety that has followed me from a young age, it is resilience that I need in order to make sure I don't catastrophise or wallow in self-pity. Resilience helps me to move forward positively with the day.

A case for optimism

My words may have left you feeling dispirited, but we can – and should – conclude this chapter on a note of optimism. Teaching is, of course, a challenging profession and, as I have already stated, stress and anxiety will always be a part of the job – this job that we feel so passionate about. Having worked in schools across Britain, I have yet to come across a teacher who does not care deeply about the young people they support. "Ambivalence" is not in a teacher's vocabulary. But such a high degree of personal investment can make us vulnerable to burnout.

So, just as we seek out opportunities to improve our pedagogical knowledge and understanding, we need to seek out strategies to help us find a balance between doing the very best for our students and doing the best for ourselves. We are more than aware that emotion is contagious in a classroom: when we are not the best and most calm version of ourselves, young people mirror that back to us. Challenging behaviour or a lack of focus become much more visible.

In this book, we will look at healthy and simple steps we can take to ensure that we are robust and confident in facing the challenges that teaching throws our way. Doing so will help us to be the best versions of ourselves for the young people we support.

Serene summary

There is much that can contribute to feelings of intense stress for teachers: martyrdom, pressure and ambiguity about what good teaching looks like are among the worst offenders. Building self-awareness and learning to recognise the trigger points are the first steps in establishing proactive strategies to combat stress and anxiety.

2. BUILDING RESILIENCE

Anxious anecdote

"I just wish I could cope better!" Andrew wiped away a tear, avoiding eye contact with his mentor.

"What makes you think you can't cope?" asked Susan, Andrew's mentor. She had an infuriating habit of asking endless questions. She never seemed to offer an opinion.

"Because I take everything so personally," Andrew replied, *"and feel like I'm letting down the young people I teach. I just don't think I'm going to make it as a teacher."*

Resilience has a mystique about it. It can seem like something that other, more robust people magically have, while we were missed off the list when it was being dished out. But it is a quality that can be common to all of us.

It is useful to reflect on how we feel when we are lacking in resilience. The symptoms are both physical and emotional. We struggle to think rationally and are far more prone to the fight, flight or freeze responses that are the result of stress. We might experience difficulty sleeping, extreme tiredness, aches and pains, or frequent illnesses. We might have a tendency to become anxious and irritable, with an inability to think straight and make decisions. When things do go wrong, we often catastrophise.

Plagued by doubt

One of the most insidious symptoms of a lack of resilience is doubt. The phrase "plagued by doubt" is revealing: it means to be overcome, haunted and unable to move forward. It leaves us at a standstill and prevents us from growing as teachers. We might feel pessimistic about the future, with low self-esteem and confidence. The novel *Life of Pi* by Yann Martel contains a wonderful illustration of just how limiting doubt can be: "To choose doubt as a philosophy of life is akin to choosing immobility as a means of transportation."

It is very easy to beat ourselves up for not being resilient enough, not being calm enough, not responding to stress in the *ideal* way. Such an ideal is impossible, however, and beating ourselves up merely makes us feel less in control and more anxious. But with an open mindset, we can build our capacity for resilience.

Mandela's long walk

Beneath any external displays of resilience in the face of stress and anxiety hide real grit and effort – and a set of learned tools and principles that are being applied. It is impossible to discuss the cultivation of resilience without considering the experiences of Nelson Mandela. Twenty-seven years in prison will, of course, teach you much about inner fortitude; Mandela's story speaks of the innate power of human beings to persevere in the face of adversity. In his autobiography, *Long Walk to Freedom*, he wrote:

> *"I am fundamentally an optimist. Whether that comes from nature or nurture, I cannot say. Part of being optimistic is keeping one's head pointed toward the sun, one's feet moving forward. There were many dark moments when my faith in humanity was sorely tested, but I would not and could not give myself up to despair. That way lays defeat and death."*

Mandela's words on the importance of mindset link to Daniel Goleman's reflections on hope in his book *Emotional Intelligence*:

> *"Having hope means that one will not give in to overwhelming anxiety, a defeatist attitude, or depression in the face of difficult challenges or setbacks. It is more than the sunny view that everything will turn out all right; it is believing you have the will and the way to accomplish your goals."*

Our ever-changing brains

In 2014, Bruce McEwen, head of the laboratory of neuroendocrinology at Rockefeller University in New York City, published a paper with two colleagues that explored the effects of stress on the brain. The authors provided a conclusion that should give all teachers cause for some of Mandela's optimism. Here is an extract:

> *"Beyond recognizing resilience as 'achieving a positive outcome in the face of adversity', the flexibility of the brain based upon healthy architecture emerges as a primary consideration. We have seen that brain architecture continues to show plasticity throughout adult life, and studies of gene expression and epigenetic regulation reveal a dynamic and ever-changing brain."*

The last sentence is hugely encouraging: how invigorating to discover that we have "a dynamic and ever changing brain". It speaks of our capacity to grow and develop throughout adulthood, and to challenge negative internal dialogues and exaggerations. I know that I am always quick to define myself as "an anxious person".

The concept of neuroplasticity highlights further the counterproductivity of any fixed thinking about our behaviour. Neuroplasticity is the ability of the brain to form and reorganise connections and pathways. According to the psychologist Courtney Ackerman, "the term 'neuroplasticity' was first used by Polish neuroscientist Jerzy Konorski in 1948 to describe observed changes in neuronal structure (neurons are the cells that make up our brains), although it wasn't widely used until the 1960s".[3]

Scientists used to believe that the brain was fixed and by the age of 25 we were effectively hardwired. Now, the more accepted belief is that we are *not* hardwired, and that we actually have the capacity to *rewire* aspects of our brains.

Enhancing resilience

So, how do we rewire our brains to help us become more resilient? This requires a great deal of discipline and effort – it will not happen by itself. And how do we do this in the context of our work in education? Is it just about positive thinking?

The clinical psychologist Meg Jay has spent two decades studying adult development, exploring the concept of resilience and how we bounce back after experiencing challenges. In her book *Supernormal*, she discusses resilience as a heroic struggle. "It's really a battle, not a bounce," she writes, going on to argue that building and maintaining resilience is an ongoing process.

We need to apply the same focus to our mental abilities that we would to our physical abilities if we wished to become fitter. In order to deepen understanding of our own resilience, we need to begin to think about our emotional responses throughout our working day. In Part II of this book, we will explores a variety of strategies that can contribute to the development of a more resilient mindset. But, just as we would try to build one aspect of our physical fitness at a time, it is important to see building resilience as a process and focus on just one strategy at a time.

Lower levels of perfectionism tend to predict resilience, so we must let go of the pursuit of perfection (which is unachievable, anyway). We must instead embark on the pursuit of resilience with an open and optimistic mindset. The wisdom of the former US first lady Eleanor Roosevelt is apt here:

---

3   www.positivepsychology.com/neuroplasticity

"You gain strength, courage and confidence by every experience in which you really stop to look fear in the face. You are able to say to yourself, 'I have lived through this horror. I can take the next thing that comes along.' You must do the thing you think you cannot do."

Resilience questionnaire

The first step in building our resilience is becoming self-aware. The following questionnaire should provide you with a clear picture of your current levels of resilience. This is important in understanding exactly what you need to do to develop your resilience within a school-based context. It will give focus to the chapters that follow, as you see exactly which areas of your professional life might benefit from further reflection.

For each question, score yourself between 1 and 5, where 1 means "strongly disagree" and 5 means "strongly agree".

When I face a challenge, I turn at once to what can be done to put things right.	
I influence where I can, rather than worrying about what I can't influence.	
I don't take criticism of my teaching personally.	
I generally manage to keep things in my professional life in perspective.	
I am calm when things go wrong in my classroom or behaviour deteriorates.	
I'm good at finding solutions to problems.	
I wouldn't describe myself as anxious in my teaching role.	
I don't tend to avoid conflict.	
I try to control events rather than being a victim of circumstances.	
I trust my intuition.	
I manage my stress levels well.	
I feel confident and secure in my role in education.	

The more 5s that appear in your scores, the more resilient you are in your work in school. If you scored all 5s then please get in touch and tell me your secrets! For most of us, there will be questions that received lower scores. These tell us the areas that we need to work proactively to develop as we journey through this book.

Core motivations

One thing that will help us to persevere through the inevitable setbacks we will face in teaching is reflecting on our core motivation for going into education. That intrinsic motivation is different for all teachers, but there might be a degree of commonality in the essential philosophy: a passion for learning or for a particular subject; a passion for working with young people and seeing them flourish. When we lose sight of our core motivation, we can slide into apathy and resentment, and forget the optimism and sense of purpose that we felt when first stepping into a classroom.

Frequently returning to that core motivation can sustain us when things get tough. When we look back at where we started, we can see the steps we have made towards becoming the teacher we want to be. We can recognise that we are having a positive impact on lives on a daily basis. It might not be a "transformative" impact – the young people might not be dancing on the desks – but the benefits will be there.

Staying open-minded and holding on to a belief in your capacity to change, grow and develop are essential to getting the most out of the following chapters. Your own ability to thrive in the classroom will change as a result. The words of the Roman statesman Seneca show us that when it comes to our mindsets, change comes from within, not without:

> *"If you really want to escape the things that harass you, what you're needing is not to be in a different place, but to be a different person."*

Serene summary

The latest scientific research teaches us that resilience is not a fixed quality, but something we can all build and improve upon. Mindset is an essential part of that process: believing that we have the ability to develop will help us to achieve changes.

PART II: MINDSET

'No man is free who is not master of himself'
Epictetus

3. SELF-TALK

Anxious anecdote

Kevin is a science teacher and five years into his teaching career. Three of his lessons on this particular day have been excellent, with engaged students showing improved understanding. At the close of one of these lessons, a student beams at Kevin and utters the line all teachers dream of hearing: "I loved that lesson, Sir – it was so interesting!"

At lunchtime, however, things take what Kevin perceives to be a disastrous turn. The head of department pops his head around the door as Kevin is wrestling with his ill-advised tuna wrap and attempting to finish marking the mock exams.

"Kevin, the deadline for the mock exams was this morning. Your data hasn't been uploaded to the spreadsheet – can you please make it a priority?"

Suddenly, there is a knot in Kevin's stomach. Panic overtakes him. The deadline is tomorrow, isn't it?

Before he can wipe away the remains of the tuna wrap, let alone begin to upload his students' results to the dreaded spreadsheet, his next class bounds through the door. The lesson, while not matching the focus and engagement of the previous three, passes uneventfully.

On his drive home, Kevin is filled with self-loathing. His mind is dominated by exaggerated ideas of the head of department's anger and frustration with him. He is haunted by visions of an email summoning him to a "conversation at the end of the day", followed by his P45 landing on his desk.

The anthemic tones of Bruce Springsteen are drowned out by the torrent of internal criticism and agitation. The words "born to run" take on a prophetic quality and thoughts of leaving teaching again appear in Kevin's mind...

Our minds are immensely complex and powerful. Their thought patterns and biases have the capacity to completely direct how we are feeling and, indeed, our behaviour. A day spent trying to dispassionately monitor what happens in our minds can be very revealing. It can make for disturbing, *Truman Show-*

style viewing: we watch as our thoughts twist and turn, and jump from one thing to another.

A realisation that arises from this thought experiment is just how often our thoughts veer towards the negative. As John Milton wrote in his 17th-century classic *Paradise Lost*, "The mind is its own place, and in itself can make a heaven of hell, a hell of heaven." This can manifest in different ways: it is common to find ourselves internally passing judgement on others, or reflecting negatively on situations we are involved with.

These thoughts are often so automatic that we don't seek to challenge them, yet they have a significant influence on how we feel from day to day. Rarely, if ever, do we take the time to pause and question whether our interpretation of the situation is accurate. But tackling this inner voice is an important starting point in fostering resilience. We need to put on our own oxygen mask before we can be of any help to others – this has become something of a cliché, but it is entirely apt in an exploration of resilience.

The negativity spiral

Every day in school, we experience highs and lows, all of which have an emotional impact at the time. Yet which are the moments that we ruminate on? How often do memories of profound pleasure and joy (for example, Kevin's student offering recognition and thanks for the interesting lesson) fade as we turn over the challenging or negative moments in our minds? At the close of each day, do we more often judge ourselves for our failures than for our achievements?

Falling into this trap of obsessive reflection on our weaknesses serves only to intensify feelings of anxiety and stress. It ultimately increases the fear we feel and leaves us feeling pessimistic about our own capabilities. Kevin is an example of someone whose anxiety is causing him to be threat-conscious and fearful. As the Greek philosopher Epictetus, a Stoic, wrote, "Men are disturbed not by events, but by their opinion about events." With a more resilient mindset, Kevin would be able to appreciate that he had merely made a slight error of timing and recognise that the problem can be easily fixed.

Negativity bias

This inclination towards the negative can be explained by the way our brains are wired. If we understand our natural tendencies, we can work to make space for reflections that give us momentum, passion and joy.

In cognitive science, this dominance of the negative over the positive has a delightfully obvious title: negativity bias. We can thank our cave-dwelling ancestors for our inclination towards pessimism. According to psychologists, we are predisposed to be alert to aspects of our environments that could harm us.

It makes perfect sense: if our ancestors had stopped to dreamily ponder the beauty of a flower just as a predator spotted them, the consequences would have been dire. But although our sensitivity to threat was remarkably helpful at that time, these days our systems are overstimulated by the huge number of threats that surround us (although, fortunately, these perils are rarely life-threatening). Not only do we register negative stimuli much more readily than we do positive, but we also dwell on these negative events and let the more positive ones drift away. Among other things, the negativity bias explains why we do the following:

1. Fixate on negative comments and feedback, rather than the positive. Remember that lesson observation that was full of glittering praise? You registered the praise at the time, but the last-minute questions about your approach to differentiation became a fixation for weeks.
2. Respond both physically and emotionally to adverse stimuli. The increased heart rate and tightening of the muscles can be blamed in part on the negativity bias.
3. Forget pleasant experiences quickly, but continue to recall challenging experiences and traumatic events. Post-traumatic stress disorder is an extreme example of this: minds are haunted by the traumatic experience and unable to detach from it.
4. Channel our attention towards negative rather than positive information. This is illustrated by what we consider to be newsworthy, and by the dominance of negativity on social media. We have an almost insatiable need for negative news.

For teachers, this fixation on the negative can lead to a hugely dissatisfying professional experience. We feel inadequate as we focus on negative aspects of our lessons (which are inevitable); we find it hard to accept and act on constructive feedback. Our negativity bias can even influence how well we build relationships with our colleagues. Our ways of thinking and working become less collegiate and more individualised. As we shall see later, this tunnel vision is the enemy of resilience – more human connection is what we really need.

We are all familiar with the staffroom snipers whose relentless negativity saps the joy and optimism out of any situation. Unless we fight back against this inclination towards negativity, we risk a career marred by dissatisfaction. Not only that, but we also risk it tarnishing the experiences of our students. Young people do not want to be taught by a pessimist. They want the energy, drive and proactive mindset of an optimist; they want someone who is emotionally resilient.

Those staffroom snipers are likely to be stuck in a negative loop – one that clouds their perceptions of everything they come across. Luckily for us, this default mode of cognition can be altered. As we shall see, we can reprogramme our biases and shift our focus (and thinking) towards the positive.

Self-compassion

Compassion is a term we are all familiar with. The psychologist Paul Gilbert, founder of the Compassionate Mind Foundation, defines compassion as "a sensitivity to suffering in self and others with a commitment to try to alleviate and prevent it". Interestingly, his definition goes beyond an awareness of suffering and encompasses proactive steps to try to stop it.

As teachers, compassion is very much central to our practice: we strive to behave compassionately towards young people and our colleagues. We are conscious of doing all we can to be patient, caring and support those around us to achieve their best. But the fact is that we cannot be all things to all people, even though we invest significant emotional energy in trying to do so.

And although we might behave compassionately towards others in our work in schools, the notion of self-compassion is much more alien – and self-compassion is often much harder to practise. But we need to be as committed to alleviating and preventing our own suffering as we are to that of others.

When I was first introduced to the concept of self-compassion, to say I was sceptical would be an understatement. I was pretty wedded to my negative inner monologue. When things didn't work out how I wanted them to, I would give myself an inner Muhammad Ali-style beating. Even my running habit led to inner pummellings when I was (literally) not up to speed.

I imagined that self-compassion would involve giving myself some kind of elaborate self-cuddle, or penning myself a soppy love letter. Would embracing self-compassion signal the end of my drive and motivation, and instead lead me to drift through the world upon a delicate cloud of ambivalence? Would the friends I grew up with in the Highlands of Scotland (all the stereotypes of long-haired, kilt-wearing, caber-tossing, sheep-wrestling virility are, of course, correct) scoff and mock my lack of "masculinity" if I become a proponent of self-compassion?

There is, of course, a balance to be found. Neither the inner Muhammad Ali-style beating nor the delicate cloud of ambivalence are productive models of behaviour, professional or otherwise.

Finding the balance

The reality is that self-compassion isn't about rejecting responsibility or wallowing in self-pity. Instead, it is about treating ourselves with the same kindness that we would show to others. That is a sentence that is easy to write, but the sentiment is much harder to live out, because most of us have been trained in this inner monologue from childhood. Like any habit, it is difficult to break. As Gilbert told me when I interviewed him for my podcast *The Well Teacher*,[4] developing compassion for ourselves makes us more self-aware:

> *"When we are compassionate to ourselves, we are able to acknowledge these understandable reactions and, rather than push them away or stop feeling what is genuine within us, learn how to tolerate, bear and manage them without ruminating on or amplifying them."*

For teachers, whose emotional radar is incredibly important to building relationships and supporting learning, this description of working with negative emotions is very helpful. So, how do we start to put this practice of self-compassion into place?

Reframing situations

There will never be a day in which things go perfectly in school. There will always be challenges to deal with, difficult conversations to be had and plans that go awry. Mistakes will be made – we are only human. Our negativity bias means that our internal monologue often sounds something like this:

- "That lesson was a complete disaster."
- "Why won't they behave for me?"
- "I am never going to pass this observation."
- "Why do all my students hate me?"
- "I'm such an idiot."
- "Other teachers are so much better than me."
- "I can't cope."

The unfortunate thing is that these thoughts can become a self-fulfilling prophecy, while our negative perceptions of our ability can have an impact on our behaviour. Confidence in the classroom is such a fragile thing and young people can see when we have lost it.

To challenge repetitive thought patterns and keep yourself from building mistakes up into bigger issues than they actually are, try the following three steps:

---

4   https://tinyurl.com/y2talf3x

1. **Recognise.** Track your thoughts throughout the day and consider any patterns or phrases that come up repeatedly. What tone do you take in this inner monologue? Which words do you use frequently? Is self-judgement the most obvious force and could this be replaced with self-kindness? This process requires objectivity: do not fall into the trap of judging your thinking, but merely watch it.

2. **Soften.** Now ask yourself an important question: would you speak to a friend or family member in the way you are speaking to yourself? If the answer is no, it is important to ask yourself why. We need to accept the emotions that we are feeling, not fight against them or ruminate painfully upon them. The thought is out of our control: we didn't invite it to the mind party, it crept in by itself. Such detachment can keep us from emotionally investing in negative thought patterns and giving too much weight to those thoughts.

3. **Repetitive practice.** This is the real challenge. Remember that your brain has programmed itself to have negative thoughts on a loop. Every time the tendency arises to perceive a situation negatively, offer an alternative phrase or statement that works for you. One that I have found hugely beneficial is: "Is this helpful?" More often than not, the answer is no.

Humour as a tool

When we experience high levels of stress and anxiety, everything suddenly seems very, very serious and it can be difficult to detach ourselves from the situation. In 1930, the philosopher Bertrand Russell wrote the following in *The Conquest of Happiness*: "One of the symptoms of an approaching nervous breakdown is the belief that one's work is terribly important."

Humour is one of the best tools to deploy in order to avoid this trap, because it helps us to take ourselves less seriously. During the American Civil War, Abraham Lincoln suffered awfully: his generals failed him, sometimes miserably; his 11-year-old son died. After a terrible setback at the Battle of Fredericksburg in December 1862, he wrote, "If there is a worse place than Hell, I am in it." Yet, despite all this, Lincoln would spend evenings regaling guests to the White House with jokes and stories. He referred to laughter as "the joyful, beautiful, universal evergreen of life".

In the wonderful *Team of Rivals*, an exploration of Lincoln's presidency and the book that Barack Obama said he couldn't be without during his own presidency, Doris Kearns Goodwin highlights Lincoln's immense fortitude: "Lincoln was as calm and unruffled as the summer sea in moments of the gravest peril." She goes on to highlight that this is, in part, about being able to adapt to negative feelings, not trying to escape them:

"Mental health, contemporary psychiatrists tell us, consists of the ability to adapt to the inevitable stresses and misfortunes of life. It does not mean freedom from anxiety and depression, but only the ability to cope with these afflictions in a healthy way."

Humour also helps us to take our internal negativity and drive for perfection less seriously – we can begin to smile at just how ludicrous some of our own internal reflections are. Humour is perhaps the easiest to apply of the forms of self-compassion, as we poke gentle fun at our tendency to fixate on the negatives.

A positive-negative charter

Another useful strategy is to create a positive-negative charter. On a piece of paper, draw two columns. In the first column, write down all the negative perceptions of yourself that are repeated in your mind; in the second column, come up with a counter to each of those perceptions. This can be a very helpful visual reminder of all your positive qualities. It helps to overwrite the negative perceptions with a positive reality, and trains you into a more optimistic mindset.

The charter also allows you to be very clear on your strengths – those unique aspects that you can draw on when you experience difficulties. Being able to recognise your own strengths and utilise them is key to building resilience. If you find this process challenging, just ask the people who know you best: they may perceive strengths that you are unaware of.

Compassionate self-talk

Part of achieving a more optimistic mindset is using positive language to communicate with ourselves. There is clearly a balance to be found here: we need to acknowledge and take responsibility for errors and mistakes, but also realise that the important thing is to learn from them, not berate ourselves for them. Mistakes are a part of human nature, but with resilience we can bounce back and keep going. As Dr Kristin Neff, self-compassion researcher, author and teacher, has said,[5] "With the burnout issues teachers face, taking care of themselves through work/life balance is important, but it isn't enough. Teachers need to give themselves permission to be self-compassionate for the stress they're under."

To start with, detaching from the pernicious inner monologue will be very challenging. Writing can help. Writing in a journal, for example, challenges us to alter how we are thinking and can allow us to become more emotionally detached, providing a route out of the negative thinking that stress and anxiety encourage. Working with a coach, as we will explore later, can also help to make

---

5   https://tinyurl.com/y4qsvwov

detachment easier, because verbally expressing how we feel allows us to gain more perspective. The phrase "It's good to talk" exists for a reason!

It might be helpful to reflect on times in your past when you have demonstrated resilience. Great or small, there will be some adversity that you have triumphed over. You might have faced a difficult class, student or colleague. You might have needed considerable perseverance to get your teaching degree in the first place! Holding on to that experience of overcoming adversity can give you confidence and show you that you can, in fact, cope with stress and move forward positively. The reality is that we all need challenges in our lives to make us stronger and more robust in the future.

Another useful phrase to apply in stressful situations is: "This will pass." All things are fleeting, no matter how disastrous they feel at the time. Try to imagine a future where this stressful moment will not matter so much – this can reduce the intensity of the distress. You might ask yourself one of these questions:

- How will I feel when I reflect on this?
- Will this matter in a few years' time?

Taking this long view helps us to perceive the situation in a clearer and less emotional way, and encourages us to see it as a learning opportunity. Once we begin to get into this habit of reframing negatives as opportunities to learn and develop, then it is easier to build this into our inner monologue.

Naming the voice that tries so hard to put a negative spin on daily events can help us to detach further. There is potential here for playfulness: Anxious Andy, perhaps? We can come to see these intrusions as those of an unwelcome visitor whom we have the power to silence.

Then it is about finding phrases that you feel comfortable with. These could range from "Everything will be OK" to "You have made a mistake" and "What is the worst that could happen?" Recognition of motivation and intent is important – it is likely that there was nothing intentional in any errors or mistakes you have made. Challenging negative perceptions with an internal "I am trying my hardest" might help.

We have to step off the treadmill of perfectionism that is so often promoted by our social media society. Despite what appearances might suggest, we all make mistakes and perfection is literally impossible. Just reminding ourselves of this fact can help immeasurably.

Losing our edge?

For those who cry that this altered mindset will lead to an acceptance of errors and a decline in performance, the research appears to suggest otherwise. In a paper, "The role of self-compassion in development: a healthier way to relate to oneself", Neff writes: "Because self-compassionate individuals do not berate themselves when they fail, they are more able to admit mistakes, modify unproductive behaviors and take on new challenges."

Heightened feelings of stress often freeze us and prevent us from taking on responsibility and engaging more fully with the world. The reality is that the negative internal monologue is not enabling us to be better, but is constricting us. Rather than making us lose our "edge", self-compassion helps us to feel more positive about our work and aids the prevention of stress, anxiety and, ultimately, burnout. By cultivating self-compassion, we also learn to say no. We learn to recognise when we are working in a way that is not productive for ourselves or the people around us.

This is not about looking through rose-tinted glasses. It is about recognising that what we have done before may have contributed to us feeling unhappy and ineffective. We need to learn to accept how we are feeling and not fight against it. When we do this, the harsh self-judgement begins to be quietened.

Serene summary

Rather than rejecting self-compassion as a narcissistic symptom of "Generation Me", it is important to see it as a way of becoming more effective and robust in our work in schools. Regular practice of self-compassion will help us to understand that we are always going to be learning, growing and improving in our personal and professional lives. Self-compassion can also make us more compassionate and understanding of others – an essential quality when working with young people.

4. GRATITUDE

Anxious anecdote

It had been a Monday that Emily hoped to quickly forget, one shrouded in a fog of tiredness. The night before had, again, been full of tossing and turning and fretting about the busy week ahead. It seemed like an impossible combination to manage: a parents' evening, a shedload of marking and yet another data collection to complete.

Before leaving school, Emily made the obligatory check of her pigeonhole. Its redundancy never seemed to be recognised; it was a relic from the past, yet it clung on against the rising tide of emails. But today, surprisingly, Emily's pigeonhole contained a letter addressed to "Miss Henderson". Intrigued, she read the opening paragraph:

"I am writing to thank you for all the support and help you have given me in the past year. I have always really struggled with maths, but you were so patient with us as a class (even, somehow, with David) and explained everything so well. You really care about maths as a subject and I felt like you always made time for me. I will always be grateful for that."

Emily looked around her, blinking hard to suppress tears. This student had barely said a word to her, yet, in this one paragraph, they had validated what had felt like a long and challenging year.

I want to tell you the story of how I came to appreciate the power of gratitude. It is a very personal one and it starts with a transition to a new school.

Moving schools is, without doubt, highly stressful for teachers: the familiarity, routine and established relationships are all left behind as we step into the unknown. After five years of teaching in London, I found my first year in a new school in the North East of England a real battle. But this wasn't down to the school itself, which was full of wonderful staff and pupils.

My experience at my previous school – where I had taken on a leadership position that required me to be a version of myself I was never comfortable with – seemed to have completely altered how I felt and behaved in school. After I had burnt out quite spectacularly and handed in my notice in the January of the previous academic year, I had faced six months of stressful and unpleasant experiences in that school.

In chapter 17, I will unpick the ramifications of toxic schools and environments. The reality is that they can have lasting consequences, emotionally and physically, for teachers and for students. Some schools function in ways that are anything but healthy, and it is profoundly important for us to talk about this as a profession.

Distorted perspectives

During this first year at my new school, I really struggled. I would wake up every day at 4am in a state of utter panic. I found it difficult to cope with the changes and felt like I couldn't think clearly.

There was nothing unusually stressful about my work in this new school: I had left behind all leadership responsibility and returned to classroom teaching. Yet even the smallest provocation would inspire a flood of anxiety – I was completely without emotional resilience. The fact that the school had just been placed in special measures added to the anxiety. There was much dissatisfaction about the changes that inevitably had to be made, and fear of Ofsted haunted every decision.

I was confused about the way my mind was responding. I was experiencing a vicious circle of internal criticism: I had struggled to cope in a demanding leadership role; now I couldn't cope as a classroom teacher? When people experiencing mental health difficulties talk about living in a fog, it is entirely apt. I was not able to see beyond this murky perspective and I felt utterly lost. My mind was programmed to perceive things negatively.

I followed the "masculine" stereotype in my attitude towards dealing with mental health difficulties. I buried my head in the sand and was convinced there was nothing wrong with me. I even applied for a leadership position in a different school, believing it was the loss of responsibility that was affecting my self-esteem. I blamed others and looked at everything other than myself and how I was feeling.

Only later did I realise that I was experiencing something akin to post-traumatic stress. The intense anxiety was, in fact, how I had been feeling in school for a long time, and I was bringing these learned behaviours to my new environment. Eventually, my wife talked me into seeing a therapist. I cannot overestimate the importance of seeking professional help if you are experiencing difficulties with your mental health. For me, it was difficult but transformative.

At the end of a long year of battling these various issues, I questioned whether I could go on with teaching. I felt drained. Exhausted. The challenge of maintaining a "front" had left me without confidence. This is why I am now so passionate about the importance of resilience for teachers – it really is integral to thriving in the profession. Without resilience, I would argue that teaching is too challenging to cope with: our roles are too public and we have to be too sensitive to the needs of others to maintain a front for long without burning out.

Discovering gratitude

That summer, I was using one of my early morning awakenings to surreptitiously raid the bookshelf of a friend I was staying with. One book caught my eye: *Gratitude* by Oliver Sacks. I tore through this collection of essays, written by Sacks at the close of his life, in just a couple of hours and it really moved me (tears were shed).

Sacks was 81 when he was diagnosed with liver cancer and told he had only months left to live. The following extract has appeared in all three of the books I have written, highlighting just how transformative Sacks' words were for me. They helped me to see that I had lost this capacity to recognise and celebrate what was good in my own life:

> "I cannot pretend I am without fear. But my predominant feeling is one of gratitude. I have loved and been loved; I have been given much and I have given something in return; I have read and travelled and thought and written. I have had an intercourse with the world, the special intercourse of writers and readers.
>
> Above all, I have been a sentient being, a thinking animal, on this beautiful planet, and that in itself has been an enormous privilege and adventure."

Before reading Sacks' book, I hadn't really engaged with the notion of gratitude in a deliberate way. If anything, I felt it was a bit schmaltzy and superficial. And it's true that "gratitude" can feel condescending or inappropriate when it is forced. When you are locked in a toxic school, to take an educational example, that is not the time to be expressing gratitude – it is the time to leave! Yet, when we start to see gratitude as something that can help us to tackle anxiety and stress, we begin to appreciate how it can enrich our lives and support inner balance.

Later in the same essay, Sacks writes of his intention to use his final months to "live in the richest, deepest, most productive way I can". That summer, I more or less stole Sacks' wisdom and set up my first blog: teachergratitude.com. The aim of this was to express gratitude for the joys of teaching – to pause at the end of every week and write about something in my professional life for which I was grateful.

Predictably, for months I had a readership that it would be generous to deem miniscule. This idealistic nugget from my first ever blog post, "The joys of English teaching", gives some indication why:

> *"Every day we communicate with a diverse range of young people,*
> *who each bring their own unique vision of the world. Sometimes it is*
> *important to remind ourselves what a genuine privilege this is, something*
> *we should feel immensely grateful for. Young people are inevitably*
> *frustrating, capricious and exhausting, but they are also wonderful – in*
> *their many guises, in their fascinating views, in their diverse humour, in*
> *their idealistic desire to make a difference in the world. It is a cliché but*
> *true: young people make sure that no day in teaching is exactly the same."*

I am not a natural writer and the laborious process of trying to bring coherence to my ramblings began to change how I perceived teaching as a profession, helping me to recognise the positives of my work. This was not an easy transition and it still isn't. My previous school experience had almost indoctrinated me into seeing only the flaws and the threat section of my brain was running on overdrive. I was, however, slowly altering my perspective on working in a school – I was beginning to see it as something that could be joyful and fulfilling, rather than stressful and anxiety-inducing.

Not that I realised it at the time, but this gratitude "habit" was also making me more resilient and less fixated on the anxiety I was experiencing. It was making me more open and creative; more willing to experiment and try new things. I was more inclined to ask for help and to move away from the perfectionism that had previously dominated my work.

As Alex Korb writes in his book *The Upward Spiral*, gratitude can be one way to step out of the negativity loop: "Gratitude can have such a powerful impact on your life because it engages your brain in a virtuous cycle. Your brain only has so much power to focus its attention. It cannot easily focus on both positive and negative stimuli."

A year of gratitude trained me to think more optimistically; to see beyond the petty frustrations of my week and recognise the good things. This is not something I have perfected; it is a practice that I work consciously on. The aim is to make sure that I do not blind myself to the positives of teaching.

How to be grateful

"Count your blessings", that familiar mantra of our parents and grandparents, is steeped in philosophical argument about how to live a positive life. The Stoic philosophers taught noble acceptance of what we have in life. The words of Seneca encapsulate this: "True happiness is to enjoy the present, without anxious dependence upon the future, not to amuse ourselves with either hopes or fears but to rest satisfied with what we have, which is sufficient, for he that is so wants nothing."

Gratitude has also been a fundamental focus of religions including Buddhism, Christianity, Judaism and Islam. Wouldn't it be delightful to channel the perspective of Buddha for a day or two: "You have no cause for anything but gratitude and joy." I'm not entirely sure things would seem that way with a rowdy class of 13-year-olds last thing on a Friday, but it's a noble intention nevertheless.

Forcing ourselves to "be grateful" is clearly unrealistic and will only generate waves of inner criticism: "Why am I always so miserable? Why can't I be more optimistic?" It will also remind us of the enforced gratitude that we resented as children: remember having to write all those thank-you letters on receipt of gifts?

A habit is more likely to form if it is easily implemented and repeated over a sustained period of time. Writing down two or three things that have gone well at the end of each day can be one way to achieve this. It takes five minutes and closes the day positively. Set the focus by starting with the sentence "Today I am grateful for…". Doing this slowly and without pressure means that it will be an enjoyable and pleasurable experience – one you will be more likely to repeat.

If you can't think of anything to write, try asking the question "What am I grateful for right here, right now?" This usually bears fruit. Channel the spirit of this beautiful quotation from Maya Angelou: "This is a wonderful day. I've never seen this one before." It is a reminder that every day is full of new opportunities and things to reflect on.

After repeating this process for two weeks, you start to mentally file away positive things to write about, rather than storing up things to be anxious about. Even on difficult days, you see that there is always some sort of silver lining.

In my own journal, I end each entry with what I call a gratitude pause, where I stop and conclude in a positive way. Anne Frank, that most famous of diarists, is a fascinating example of someone who found the positives even in the most challenging of circumstances: "Beauty remains, even in misfortune. If you just look for it, you discover more and more happiness and regain your balance."

Once the gratitude habit is formed, it can be useful to move to a weekly practice. You might allow more time to explore in detail the things you are grateful for, but I would avoid trying to hit a particular target like writing five things. Instead, just one thing a week might stand out and it doesn't need to be profound. That one thing might make you feel more positive about your work, providing sustenance when things are challenging.

Recognising others

We are all interdependent. We do not operate alone in isolated bubbles and classrooms. Everything we do is the result of something that has come before, and gratitude helps us to see all the factors that influence our own work and lives.

Recognising and expressing gratitude towards others – as Emily's student did in the Anxious Anecdote that opened this chapter – can be hugely powerful. The organisational psychologist Adam Grant spent a week "writing emails to the 100 people who mattered most in my life, telling them what I appreciated most about them". Grant said, "It's one of the most meaningful things I've ever done. And it taught me something about what I valued: the two most common themes were generosity and originality."[6] We can do a similar (but less time-consuming!) thing by seeking out an individual every so often and recognising what they have done to support us in our professional roles. This can be beneficial for us and them.

Grateful schools

Having finally made it back to my native Scotland in an educational odyssey across the UK, I now teach in a comprehensive in central Edinburgh. Every Friday at break, the headteacher comes to the staffroom for one simple purpose: to say thank you. She often has a long list of people to thank for specific things; she recognises their value and shows appreciation for their efforts. This gratitude is undoubtedly contagious – it encourages positivity and gratitude in others. I have never worked in another school where this is so visible: staff thank each other and acknowledge things that have helped them all the time.

In her book *High Challenge, Low Threat*, Mary Myatt devotes a chapter to gratitude, highlighting its power to support positive relationships in schools. She writes:

> *"The most valuable resource which leaders have are their colleagues. So they express gratitude to them. They say thank you, and often. But the thanks are not cheap, off-the-cuff platitudes. They are deep and heartfelt and they come from noticing. Noticing is one of the most powerful things that thoughtful leaders do. They notice the small stuff, the things that make a person tick, the small triumphs and gains."*

Modelling gratitude

The reciprocal nature of gratitude is evident when it comes to lessons. Expressing gratitude to young people – thanking them for their contributions,

---

6   https://tinyurl.com/y6pdzwkm

for example – lays the foundations for positive and meaningful relationships. In that kind of environment, receiving that longed-for "Thank you" at the close of a lesson, or indeed a card at the end of the year, is a bit more likely.

Taking practical steps to make space for gratitude and build a resilient mindset will not result in the instant dissipation of all feelings of anxiety. It will, however, support positive thinking and help us to recognise the good. In the words of Marcus Aurelius, "Dwell on the beauty of life. Watch the stars and see yourself running with them."

Serene summary

To help counter feelings of anxiety, start by writing down three things for which you feel grateful at the close of each day. Then start a weekly journal in which you take time to consider the positives that can be drawn from that week. Roll with this momentum and begin to express gratitude to the people around you for all that they help you to achieve and do. In your teaching, try to model to young people the value and importance of gratitude.

5. SUPPORTING OTHERS

Anxious anecdote

"Feelgood Friday" was not an event that Henry shared with his students or colleagues. Every Thursday, he began to plan who would be the recipient of that week's act of kindness. The purpose was simple: to raise a smile.

On this Friday, he placed an unsigned postcard and a chocolate bar on his colleague Helen's desk. She had been struggling recently with challenging classes and problems at home. The postcard read: "You are stronger than you think – I admire you so much. Keep going."

The principles of altruism and kindness are at the core of Matthieu Ricard's life. As a young Frenchman with a promising scientific career, he left it all behind to move to the Himalayas and practise Tibetan Buddhism. He completely immersed himself, becoming a Buddhist monk and humanitarian.

Many years later, he took part in intensive clinical tests at the University of Wisconsin; his brain patterns were monitored and the scans revealed unusually high levels of "happiness" activity (gamma waves). The results led to a new reputation in the media as "the world's happiest man".

The secret to happiness, according to Ricard, is altruism. "It's not the moral ground," Ricard told *Business Insider*.[7] "It's simply that me, me, me all day long is very stuffy. And it's quite miserable, because you instrumentalise the whole world as a threat, or as a potential source of interest [to yourself]." His argument that self-interest can prevent us from being happy is made even clearer in his book *Altruism*:

> *"By breaking down our sense of self-importance, all we lose is a parasite that has long infected our minds. What we gain in return is freedom, openness of mind, spontaneity, simplicity, altruism: all qualities inherent in happiness."*

---

7   https://tinyurl.com/y5z3f7xx

That sounds pretty delightful. But how can we apply altruism in a professional context? And can it really boost our wellbeing and resilience?

Altruism and community

Having read Ricard's book (at almost 1000 pages long, it is an epic read!), I'm not certain that there is such a thing as an entirely selfless act. Do we really behave in selfless ways in order to benefit others? In many ways, however, the debate is pointless: the motivations are less important than the impact our choices and behaviour have on other people.

Altruism is a conscious choice – one that requires us to place the wellbeing of others before our own. The word itself derives from the Latin *alter*, meaning "other", and it was popularised by Auguste Comte, the French philosopher and founder of positivism, in the 19th century.[8] His definition is an interesting place to start: "The elimination of selfish desire and of egocentrism, as well as living a life devoted to the wellbeing of others."

With all the pressure that teachers experience, it can be difficult to move beyond the immediate classroom environment and the detailed, individualised thinking required. That is not meant as a criticism: the reality is that teachers are often placed in competition with each other, rather than being expected to work collegiately for the greater good.

The decline of the staffroom – with the communication and community it represents – is a worrying example of this. Some newly built schools don't even have a staffroom, as evidenced by this article in *The Guardian*:[9]

> "*Anish Mann, a physics teacher, recently left a school, part of a multi-academy trust, that had no staffroom. As a result, he says, he only got to know his department team, not the whole staff. He says: 'I would see adults walking in the school and would challenge them on their ID. We all thought it was a divide and conquer situation. If you don't let people talk to each other, they don't share their grievances.'*"

A fixation on individual teachers' exam results, alongside performance-related pay and promotion based on results, can further the dog-eat-dog ethos. Yet all this breeds a self-interest that exacerbates anxiety and makes us less happy in our profession. Throughout history it has been understood that mankind needs society and the interaction that comes with it. Aristotle's famous statement seems all the more relevant in our modern, fragmented

---

8   www.etymonline.com
9   www.theguardian.com/education/2018/mar/13/school-staffroom-england

world: "Man is a social animal." The negative effects of the Covid-19 lockdown and quarantine measures are a powerful illustration of just how much we need people in our lives.

Even if our schools have no staffrooms, however, we still have the autonomy to build relationships and offer support to others. In turn, we will be much more likely to find that the people we work with provide help and support when we need them.

Martin Luther King Jr knew how to deliver a memorable line and this quotation provides some stiff competition to his "I have a dream" speech: "Every man must decide whether he will walk in the light of creative altruism or in the darkness of destructive selfishness." In the context of a discussion of how we can bring more altruism into our professional environments, his words are illuminating.

A year of living kindly

Towards the end of 2019, I began to experience the stronger feelings of stress and anxiety that always leave me caught up in myself. I was trying to get to grips with the Scottish curriculum while teaching a full-time timetable; finishing the manuscript for my second book, *A Quiet Education*; hosting a podcast for *Tes* on English teaching; studying part-time for an educational doctorate; and, most importantly, trying to be a good husband and father. I was juggling far too many things and feeling overwhelmed.

As the new year dawned, I knew I had to make some changes. The doctorate was proving a huge challenge to fit in and I wasn't convinced it was going to have the positive impact I wanted it to. Anxiety always makes me want to do more, achieve more and move at a hundred miles an hour. It obviously, at times, has the opposite result: the more I take on, the more stressed-out I feel and the less effective I become. So, when I finally sent off the manuscript for *A Quiet Education*, I decided that I would reconsider how I used my time, with the aim of reframing my thinking and putting other people's needs before my own.

I dropped out of the doctorate and stopped doing the podcast for *Tes*. And I used some of the time this created to volunteer for two charities in the Edinburgh area: Vintage Vibes and Health in Mind. That involved spending an hour a week with an elderly and isolated person in the community, and facilitating a drop-in anxiety and depression support group once a fortnight. I also started my own podcast with a focus on wellbeing, *The Well Teacher*.[10]

I started to see beyond myself and began to look for further ways in which to help others. When the Covid-19 lockdown began, I went on a mission with

---

10 www.slowteaching.co.uk/category/the-well-teacher-podcast

my toddler son to do positive things and galvanise our local community. We delivered Easter eggs to the people on our street; we got the community to come together and write cards for people in the local care home. I also helped to set up a national creative writing competition for young people aged 7-17, Generation Lockdown Writes,[11] which received more than 5000 entries and will hopefully raise a significant amount of money for charity.

Of course, altruism is not a magical cure for feelings of anxiety. Yet anxiety often means we become stuck in our own self-narratives. At the peak of lockdown, *The New York Times* published an article called "The science of helping out",[12] which contains the following nugget:

> *"Our bodies and minds benefit in a variety of ways when we help others. Some research has focused on the 'helper's high.' Studies show that volunteering, donating money, or even just thinking about donating money can release feel-good brain chemicals and activate the part of the brain stimulated by the pleasures of food and sex. Studies of volunteers show that do-gooders had lower levels of the stress hormone cortisol on days they did volunteer work."*

We prosper – physically, mentally, emotionally – through the simple act of giving. But being altruistic does not mean being a martyr and putting others first at our own expense. We need to strike a delicate balance between self-preservation, selflessness and selfishness. By connecting with and supporting others around us, however, we are much more inclined to act in the self-compassionate manner that we explored in the previous chapter.

Geoff Barton, a former head and now general secretary of the Association of School and College Leaders, put this eloquently in an article for *Tes*:[13]

> *"In public life, we don't speak enough about the importance of kindness. In these abnormal times, it is more important than ever – kindness to ourselves, and to one another. And the best places for kindness to prevail – so that the next generation can see its significance – [are] our schools and colleges."*

When we are caught up in feelings of stress and anxiety, our self-worth is gradually eroded. Our self-narrative becomes that we are worthless, we can't

---

11   https://generationlockdown.co.uk
12   www.nytimes.com/2020/04/09/well/mind/coronavirus-resilience-psychology-anxiety-stress-
        volunteering.html
13   www.tes.com/news/school-reopenings-mental-health-must-be-top-priority

cope with teaching – and catastrophic thoughts begin to take over our minds. We blame ourselves and become locked in single-track thinking.

As with most mental health issues, proactive steps are required in order to regain a healthy perspective on the world around us. In a famous experiment, the psychologist Ellen Langer gave houseplants to two groups of nursing-home residents. She told one group that they were responsible for keeping the plants alive and that they could also make choices about their daily schedules. She told the other group that the staff would care for the plants and they were not given any choice in their schedules. Eighteen months later, members of the first group were more cheerful, active and alert – and, surprisingly, fewer had died.

This experiment indicates the importance of community and personal responsibility. To thrive in a school environment, we need to feel that we are part of a community – that we belong and are empowered. The support we receive and offer to those around us can be the difference between professional loneliness and isolation and a profession that functions as a community.

A kindness mindset

Ricard, when pressed by *Business Insider* on how we can move away from selfishness and towards altruism, suggested undergoing a kind of mental training:[14]

> *"With mental training, we can always bring [our level of happiness] to a different level. It's like running. If I train, I might run a marathon. I might not become an Olympic champion, but there is a huge difference between training and not training. So why should that not apply to the mind? ... There is a view that benevolence, attention, emotional balance and resilience are skills that can be trained. So, if you put them all together, you could say that happiness is a skill that can be trained."*

Actively planning for moments of altruism and kindness is a lovely thing to do – one that instantly begins to move your mindset away from negativity or anxiety. You might plan for just one moment a week in which you explicitly do something for someone else. Making yourself accountable will help to sustain the habit, as will setting up a journal in which you record and remind yourself of how you are helping others.

A wonderful quotation from the poet Rumi can remind us of why we seek to help others: "Be a lamp, a lifeboat, a ladder. Help someone's soul heal. Walk out of your house like a shepherd." Think about your natural gifts or your knowledge: what strengths can you draw upon to provide help or support to others?

---

14   https://tinyurl.com/y5z3f7xx

Kindness can also be about accepting the mistakes that others make, or it can come simply through dialogue and conversation. It is not about lowering expectations, but about appreciating that we all make mistakes and focusing on learning rather than criticism.

The kindness ripple effect

I asked on Twitter for stories of random acts of kindness between teachers and school staff. I received hundreds of responses and, for inspiration, a few are listed below. They speak of the huge opportunity we have to spread positivity and kindness – not just between staff members, but also among the young people in our schools. The examples below also demonstrate the capacity of our students to brighten our experience of teaching!

"We have a Secret Karma Club in our school. You sign up and are given the name of someone else to look after, get gifts for, etc, but all in secret."

"A few years ago I was diagnosed with a chronic illness. When I returned to school, I told my form. A week later they gave me a survival kit box which had my fave chocs in it alongside some books about my illness. Also a handmade diary for me to log my thoughts about my illness."

"In my NQT year I had a bad lesson and felt extremely frustrated. Then, a pupil stayed behind to give me a mini recipe book she had written for me because I told the class before I had all sorts of intolerances. She said she didn't want me to miss out on any nutrients."

"Teachers offering to do someone's cover because they could see that person was already having a difficult day of their own."

"Someone leaving a chocolate bar and note on my desk to say thank you for being a thoughtful teacher."

"Handwritten notes from colleagues with compliments or a positive message. Get students in your form to write a postcard to a teacher they'd like to thank each week and give them out on Friday – I love these and have treasured all mine!"

"I arrived one morning to find a beautiful bunch of tulips left on my desk one morning. Made me smile all day. Still does whenever I think about it!"

"When I got my first deputy job, the current deputy gave a deputy survival kit she'd made. Was so touched, never used it – couldn't bear to. Now make them for others."

"New school, feral, hostile Yr 11 class. Me: experienced but in despair. Found a rose on my desk and note saying: 'You are quite simply the rose amongst the thorns.' Made me laugh and feel not so alone. I relaxed: thorns didn't scratch so much."

"An anonymous member of staff gave me a card with a very thoughtful and kind message in it and a voucher to treat myself to something."

"Y11 student baked me vegan cookies (nut free!) and left them on my desk with a little card. Another GCSE student who'd given me a hard time with challenging behaviour wrote a card to apologise and promised to change her ways. She did. She wrote another to thank me when we closed."

"Secret friend club. You get little gifts throughout the year from your secret friend – you, in turn, gift someone else. My highlight was the gift box of mini gin bottles, chocolates and an escape room game that arrived during lockdown Easter. It made my day!"

"Gift from the HoD, asked students to write notes about the other teachers in the department and was given as an Xmas present. Keep it in my desk for if I'm having a bad time."

"We had a kindness week, it replaced homework. It was my favourite week at work this year! Students thrived. We also do a staff random act of kindness, like secret Santa. Empower empathy!"

In performing such random acts of kindness, the result is that we begin to move outside of ourselves. As Daniel Goleman writes in his book *Social Intelligence*:

"Self-absorption in all its forms kills empathy, let alone compassion. When we focus on ourselves, our world contracts as our problems and preoccupations loom large. But when we focus on others, our world expands. Our own problems drift to the periphery of the mind and so seem smaller, and we increase our capacity for connection – or compassionate action."

Much like gratitude, altruism becomes addictive and contagious as others start to see its impact. As the Swiss philosopher Alexandre Jollien tells Matthieu Ricard in his book *Altruism*, "Altruism is like rings in the water when you toss a pebble. At first the circles are very small, then they get larger, and finally they embrace the entire surface of the ocean."

That ripple effect can have a significant impact on our resilience levels, helping us to feel more positive, calmer and more able to cope with the challenges that we will inevitably face in our work in schools.

Serene summary

Behaving in a kind and altruistic way will benefit our health and happiness. Working to build a kindness mindset and taking small steps towards putting others first will challenge the negativity and self-absorption that is often the product of anxious thinking.

6. SELF-AWARENESS

Anxious anecdote

"Now I would like you to sit in an upright posture, close your eyes and follow your breath. You should find yourself entering a calm, tranquil state – your worries dissolving like ever-changing clouds in the wind."

Penny lifted her eyelids a little to peer at the other staff, who were all sitting rigidly still with their eyes clamped shut. Was this bloke for real? When he had walked – or floated – into the staffroom, she had felt an almost overwhelming urge to giggle.

His hair was in a ponytail, which always aroused suspicion in Penny – she couldn't help it. His unfortunate habit of leaving exaggerated pauses while he gesticulated in a ludicrous fashion made him even more like a caricature. The whale music that accompanied his "mindful introduction" had almost tipped Penny over the edge.

It was the first day back after the summer break and Penny's worries were certainly not dissolving. This "mindful hour" session was only making the situation worse. She could have used the time to prepare lesson plans, seating arrangements and resources for the next day, but instead here she was, with a mind that was anything but calm and tranquil.

Ponytail Man appeared to read her thoughts: "If you feel your mind wandering, gently and kindly guide it back to a focus on your breath." Irrational anger swelled inside Penny. There was nothing gentle or kind about how she was going to storm out of this ridiculous session!

Welcome to the infamous staff wellbeing intervention. The desperate attempts of senior leaders to pacify staff over workload concerns have led to the arrival of the "mindfulness in schools" expert. Not only will he condense thousands of years of spiritual wisdom into one hour, but he will also bring an easily applied "practical element" to the course. First, staff will collaboratively experience a short mindfulness session. Afterwards, they will be given the tools to start a mindfulness habit and develop a calmer, more easeful approach to their teaching. Soon they will have increased personal resilience, with the ability to surmount any obstacle with serene tranquillity.

Although well-intentioned, these obligatory wellbeing interventions have resulted in scepticism and resentment. A stressed and overworked community of teachers will not see a superficial mindfulness workshop as a solution – they will see it as failing spectacularly to address the root causes of the stress and anxiety they experience.

Mindfulness is not a panacea for the ills of the modern age – and it is certainly not a solution to workload issues among school staff. Yet, even though it has been oversimplified and its benefits oversold, there is much that a sustained mindfulness habit can offer teachers. As a tool to manage strong impulses and emotional responses, it can be our secret weapon in maintaining balance and developing the self-awareness necessary for resilience.

Mindfulness and me

As recent and robust scientific research has proven, mindfulness and meditation can be really effective in countering feelings of anxiety and stress. *The Science of Meditation* by Daniel Goleman and Richard Davidson offers a plethora of scientific evidence of the value of meditation. Davidson's research has demonstrated that mindfulness can build resilience, helping those who practise it regularly to "reframe stressful situations more productively". Being mindful and self-aware helps us to detach from feelings of stress. Instead of catastrophising when we face difficulties and challenges, we can see things more clearly and with greater perspective.

Although mindfulness is now hugely popular, just five years ago, when my wife came bounding back from a government training session on mindfulness, I had no idea what she was talking so enthusiastically about. I remember feeling mildly insulted as she outlined in great detail how this practice was perfect for me. The words "frazzled", "autopilot" and "struggling to cope" were used to justify why I needed to become acquainted with it.

Eventually, my mild irritation gave way to pragmatism: I knew my mind was running amok and my anxiety was proving very difficult to bring under control. I was feeling anything but resilient at that point – I was teetering on the edge. I encapsulated this statement from the 17th-century polymath Blaise Pascal: "All of humanity's problems stem from man's inability to sit quietly in a room alone."

With that nudge from my wife, I began a meditation practice that has become very important to me. It has helped me to manage my feelings of anxiety and cultivate a calmer, more positive approach to life.

What is mindfulness?

Mindfulness is rooted in the Buddhist tradition. Ultimately, it is about noticing present thoughts, feeling and sensations without judgement. The aim is a state of "bare awareness" – one that is not influenced by any other factors. A popular definition comes from Jon Kabat-Zinn, who developed the mindfulness-based stress reduction (MBSR) programme in the 1970s: "Awareness that arises through paying attention, on purpose, in the present moment, non-judgementally."[15]

"Bare awareness" means you are fully present and fully engaged with whatever you are doing at that very moment – no distractions. Our "monkey minds", however, with their tendency to leap all over the place, make bare awareness very difficult to achieve.

I have spent more time meditating as the years have gone on, and I can categorically reveal that meditation is anything but easy (meditation is the formal practice of mindfulness and can take many different forms, including mindfulness meditation). Sitting still and following your breath is just the start. Our minds and emotions do not have an "off" button.

As I write this, during lockdown, I am attempting to meditate for about an hour every day (from 6-7am, or until loudly interrupted by my toddler) to try to maintain some semblance of calm. Is this a period of blissful relaxation? Often, it very much is not. My mind is no longer as frantic as it once was, but it is still of the extremely active variety – like most teachers! Much of my meditation time is spent recognising the emotions that arise and attempting to return my focus to the breath in a non-judgemental way.

Just this morning, I "failed" miserably to achieve any sort of focus or concentration. Instead, I fixated on how I was going to manage potty-training (toddler's, not mine) alongside facilitating and supporting students' online learning, while maintaining a calm veneer in the face of tantrums (toddler's and mine).

Critics may argue that such an hour is utterly wasted, but for me it makes perfect sense and helps me to build my self-awareness. The more familiar we are with just how fickle and ungovernable our minds really are, the more we can detach ourselves emotionally. In turn, the more emotional resilience and calm we can generate.

Dan Harris, an anchor for the ABC news network in the US who had a panic attack on live TV, highlights in his book *10% Happier* the inherent challenge of a meditation practice:

---

15   www.mindful.org/jon-kabat-zinn-defining-mindfulness

"To truly tame the 'monkey mind' and defeat our habitual tendency toward clinging, meditation was the prescription, and sitting and actively facing the 'voice in your head' mindfully for a few minutes a day might be the hardest thing you'll ever do. Accept that challenge and improve your life drastically. It's about mitigation, not alleviation. It's that simple. The only way out is through."

Richard Burnett, who co-founded the Mindfulness in Schools project, told me in an episode of *The Well Teacher* podcast[16] that his morning practice was what "grounded and prepared" him for the day ahead. That doesn't result in a loss of edge. Rather, it provides a sense of focus and an understanding of how we might better use our time. And that is key. We might feel so busy that it is impossible to find time for mindfulness. But it is important to reflect on how we use our time: will practising mindfulness for 10 minutes have more impact than scrolling through social media for 10 minutes?

Meditation myths

Another argument often levelled against meditation is that it can make you lose your edge, changing you into a languid figure lacking in inner drive. But this drawing of a correlation between self-care and loss of ambition says a lot about our society. Sure, meditation can help us to become calmer, but the key difference for me has been an increased ability to concentrate and less of a propensity to be pushed around by my own conflicting emotions.

"Increased focus" has been a preoccupation of the self-help industry for a long, long time – it is a quality that we all need in this age of multitasking. That ability to remain unshaken by the events of the day can be hugely powerful when it comes to productivity. As Seneca wrote: "You may be sure that you are at peace with yourself, when no noise reaches you, when no word shakes you out of yourself, whether it be flattery or a threat, or merely an empty sound buzzing about you with unmeaning din."

Some people might also argue that meditation and mindfulness are an egotistical pursuit that helps no one but ourselves. But I would argue that making a priority of our mental health is not narcissistic or an indulgence – it is a necessity. Of course, the desire to feel less stressed, anxious and fearful is about self-compassion, but it is also about compassion for others: being better versions of ourselves for the people around us; being more present, calmer teachers for the students around us. If meditation and mindfulness can do that, then their benefits greatly outweigh the investment of time.

---

16   www.slowteaching.co.uk/2020/06/10/benefits-mindfulness-teachers-young-people

There are also many forms of meditation that seek to recognise the experiences of others and wish them well – a "loving kindness" meditation is a good example of that sort of practice. Being clear about our motivation gives our meditation meaning beyond merely quietening our minds.

Mindfulness benefits for teachers

In the book *Happy Teachers Change the World*, the Buddhist monk Thich Nhat Hanh, who was nominated for a Nobel Peace Prize in 1967 by Martin Luther King Jr, tells the story of sending a letter to a young teacher. In the letter, Nhat Hanh outlined the importance of embracing a more mindful mindset:

> *"The first step is to come back to yourself – the way out is in. Come back to yourself to be able to take care of yourself: learn how to generate a feeling of happiness; learn how to handle a painful feeling or emotion; listen to your own suffering, so that understanding and compassion can be born and you will suffer less. This is the first step and, as a teacher, you have to be able to do this."*

These words illustrate the necessity of knowing yourself in order to find inner resilience. A similar philosophy of self-care enabling our work with young people is powerfully embodied in the following quotation, from the education professor and wellbeing expert Katherine Weare:

> *"Wellbeing in schools starts with the staff: they are in the front line of this work, and it is hard for them to be genuinely motivated to promote emotional and social well-being in others if they feel uncared for and burnt out themselves."*[17]

There are three other ways in which a mindfulness and meditation habit can prove beneficial for teachers, particularly in terms of boosting our resilience:

1. Challenging behaviour, as we shall see in chapter 18, has the potential to make us feel drained and emotional. Mindfulness and meditation can help us to keep calm and manage our own emotions in difficult situations. It can also stop us from ruminating painfully and pointlessly on past and future events.

---

17 www.mentalhealth.org.nz/assets/ResourceFinder/What-works-in-promoting-social-and-emotional-wellbeing-in-schools-2015.pdf

2. Teaching often requires us to take a step back from situations and be dispassionate – another key quality that can be developed through mindfulness training. We cannot become too emotionally invested in our work with young people, or we run the risk of experiencing burnout.

3. Teachers often move through the day at a frantic pace – we are always rushing to get things done. Meditation helps us to slow down and be more measured in how we approach our interactions and our teaching.

If we could bring a little mindfulness to our teaching, our pupils would be the beneficiaries of an energy focused on that particular moment and that particular aspect of learning. We all love to be in the presence of someone who gives us their full focus and attention. Young people respect and appreciate teachers who recognise and make time for them as individuals.

For some teachers, including me, the "teacher worry" can be all-consuming: our minds anxiously revisit mistakes made in lessons, anticipate the problems that lie ahead and turn over the items on our to-do lists. But training our focus and energy on the current moment can prevent us from becoming overwhelmed. As Thich Nhat Hanh highlights, "Meditation is not evasion, it is a serene encounter with reality."

Applying mindfulness

The following steps should help to build a sustainable mindfulness habit. Do not expect to see the kind of instant results promoted at staff mindfulness sessions. As with the learning and development of all complex skills, mindfulness requires discipline and practice. Lots of us invest this sort of effort in building our physical fitness – we need to take the same approach to our mental fitness.

1. **Commit to a time**. First, make a decision about the time of day when you can commit to meditation. For some, the quiet of the morning works best and allows a positive start to the day; for others, the evening is a better time and provides closure at the end of the day. Whatever time you choose, stick with it.

2. **Commit to a place**. Once you have your designated time, find a spot that is quiet and relaxing. Particularly at the start of building a mindfulness habit, the mind looks for any and all distractions. Finding a spot that offers the least temptation possible will help you to maintain concentration.

3. **Set aside 10 minutes.** You need to be able to fit your practice into what is probably a hectic schedule (you are a teacher, after all!) and 10 minutes is an achievable amount of time. Sustaining this habit over a number of

days and then week after week will give it the best chance of becoming a part of your life. As you begin to feel the benefits, you may want to increase the time you spend on your daily practice.

4. **Begin with breathing**. There are all kinds of ways to actually *do* a mindfulness practice. The most obvious way to stay present is to track your breath. This is much harder than it sounds: it can be difficult to keep the mind focused as you follow your breathing in and out. You might want to use an app to support your practice and there are some excellent examples out there: Headspace is currently free to school staff (www.headspace.com/educators); Ten Percent Happier (www.tenpercent.com) has lots of guided meditations and talks. This habit of tracking your breath can then be transferred to moments of stress and tension throughout your day. Breathing can help you to calm down after a particularly difficult lesson and return to a more positive state before the next class arrives.

5. **Track the positives**. For any new habit to stick, we need to feel like there is a clear benefit. Meditation and mindfulness can be difficult in this regard, as there is not always an easily noticeable impact. Be reflective and carefully consider the changes you can see. Some questions to ask: have I felt less overwhelmed since I started meditating? Has there been an impact on my patience levels with others? How have my interactions been different since I took up a mindfulness practice? Have I noticed myself being more aware of what is happening around me?

Once we begin to recognise the positives, we will have a habit that is ingrained and is likely to be with us for a long time. Greg McKeown, in his book *Essentialism*, says: "Once we master [new skills] and make them automatic, we have won an enormous victory, because the skill remains with us for the rest of our lives. Once they are in place they are the gifts that keep on giving."

There is a temptation for a mindfulness habit to become yet another thing to berate ourselves about: yet another task on the to-do list and yet another thing to feel guilty about if we don't manage to do it. This is the perfect opportunity to work on the self-compassion that we explored earlier. Forgive yourself and come back to the purpose and motivation behind your practice.

Over time, you will hopefully feel less frantic and look forward to your moments of quiet, still meditation. The day that you find yourself reacting to stress and challenge in a calm and thoughtful way will be the day you know your efforts are paying off. It will also indicate that you are building up your levels of resilience. Others may recognise and comment on a change in your behaviour. And the young people you teach may find themselves enjoying the company of a more attuned, more positive and less reactive teacher.

Serene summary

Although mindfulness is not a panacea, a sustained practice has the potential to be very helpful for teachers. The key to establishing a habit is little and often. Start with 10 minutes a day. Use the time to try to build your capacity to be in the moment. Tracking the impact and keeping an open, positive mindset will keep you motivated in the long term.

7. MANAGING CONFLICT

Anxious anecdote

The meeting was disintegrating before Jen's eyes. She had expected Harold to be the first to reject the new colour-coded feedback policy – and, as predicted, he led the revolt.

"I am overworked and exhausted. I don't know how you expect me to do this."

Senior management had told her that the new marking policy had to be implemented straight away – the imminent progress inspection was going to focus on it. She had absolutely no say in the matter.

"If we work together, we will be able to manage it." Jen knew her response was superficial: marking the books would have to be done by the individual teachers. Privately, she felt the colour-coded marking was ludicrous, but she hadn't felt brave enough to voice her concerns in the management meeting.

"Are you going to mark my set of books, then? Are you going to spend hours with all these different colours?" Harold's disdain was clear for all the department to see. An awkward silence descended…

Every day, we have vital conversations with our colleagues. Some are successful and support our aim to do our best for our students. Others lead to misunderstandings, miscommunication and ultimately conflict. Responding to conflict with resilience and clarity is essential to ensure that tensions are not permitted to linger, harming our own wellbeing and that of our colleagues.

Conflict resolution, however, doesn't often feature on the training materials we receive as teachers. There are two key types of conflict that teachers may experience in the workplace, and we need strategies to cope with each.

First, we may face challenging behaviour from young people. As we shall see in chapter 18, a stoical, philosophical approach can help us to sustain a positive attitude and manage our own emotions. Second, we may experience conflict with our teaching colleagues. Although we teachers are predominately a compassionate bunch, there are tensions and disagreements in any workplace. There might be a senior member of staff who possesses few interpersonal skills, a department head who is frequently highly critical, or a colleague who is unrelentingly negative and belittles everything we do.

As with young people, teachers come in all personality types, from the extroverted to the introverted, the bombastic to the sensitive. That diversity is bound to generate some disharmony, with contrasting philosophies and ways of working. Those moments of conflict can be all the more trying after a day spent in classrooms with fickle young people: when our own emotions are heightened, small conflicts or disagreements can quickly be inflamed.

And, as schools become more results-driven, a culture of micromanagement and performativity can become more difficult to break down. Placing pressure on individuals will always lead to conflict, and teachers can resent their perceived lack of autonomy and unreasonable workload demands.

Fight or flight

In order to respond to conflict with resilience, we must learn to recognise our emotional trigger points. Daniel Goleman's book *Emotional Intelligence* is an essential read in this regard. His argument is that "emotional self-control – delaying gratification and stifling impulsiveness – underlies accomplishment of every sort". Conflict, of course, generates stress, and Goleman urges us to remember that we all have instinctive and learned emotional reactions to stress.

Walter Bradford Cannon, chair of the physiology department at Harvard Medical School, coined the term "fight or flight" in 1915 to describe an animal's response to threats. When faced with danger, the brain releases hormones like adrenaline and cortisol into the bloodstream. This rapidly leads to changes in the mind and body, such as acceleration of heart and lung action and increased muscle tension, all designed to assist our ancestors when they were in peril. So, when we experience a stress stimulus such as conflict, this evolutionary process can make us respond in ways that might not be as calm or rational as we would hope.

The simple act of acknowledging that we are responding in a biological way can help us to calm down; we recognise that we need to distance ourselves. A key strategy can be to notice the emotional triggers, name them and set them in context. The mindfulness strategies discussed in the previous chapter can be soothing and help us to become emotionally ready for a conversation. One of my favourite quotations from Marcus Aurelius is, "He who lives in harmony with himself lives in harmony with the universe." It speaks of emotional stability and how it helps us to be at peace with those around us.

We do, however, need to interrogate our motivations in situations of conflict: why are we behaving in a particular way? What outcome are we seeking? We also need to be wary of feelings of anger. As Benjamin Franklin, one of the founding fathers of the US, noted, "Anger is never without a reason, but seldom a good one."

There are a variety of strategies that we can adopt to make sure our relationships don't disintegrate as a result of conflict:

1. **Prioritise relationships**. With any form of conflict, it is important to work hard to sustain positive relationships. The reality is that we have to continue to work closely with our colleagues and prolonged conflict makes the situation uncomfortable for all. It also distracts us from our core purpose in schools: to support young people to be the best versions of themselves. Initially, we might seek to detach from difficult situations, to give ourselves the space to manage our emotional responses and think about how we can move forward positively. We might need to talk to another colleague to get advice on how best to resolve the conflict. Start with the assumption that others want to find a way forward, too. The situation might require what Kim Scott, the author of *Radical Candor: be a kick-ass boss without losing your humanity*, calls "clean escalation". "Instead of team members coming to you, the boss, to complain about each other, ask them to approach one another directly," Scott says. "If you have committed to practising radical candor – caring personally while challenging directly – as a team, this will eventually come naturally." Clean escalation does not come through sending emails. Although it might be easier to hit send than to talk it through in person, there is a real risk of making the situation worse. It is very easy to misinterpret tone in emails and it is hard to demonstrate your personal investment in the other individual. Instead, it might take some time and a number of conversations to find a resolution.

2. **Listen, then respond**. Conflict often arises through miscommunication. It is important to make the time and space to genuinely listen to those around us before we respond. We have no idea what might have influenced their behaviour; what might have happened before we had the interaction that went awry. Our lives are all complex and unpredictable, and inevitably that can influence interpersonal relationships in school. This quotation, which has been attributed to Socrates, Plato and Philo, among others, is useful here: "Be kind, for everyone you meet is fighting a hard battle." Listen to the other person and ask questions that seek to understand exactly how they are feeling. We have to appreciate how different we all are: what one person perceives as a problem or a cause of stress may not be an issue for

71

another. We must look at ourselves objectively, to see if we may be the root cause of a problem or disagreement.

3. **Keep it factual**. There is little to be gained from emotive or accusatory responses to conflict. Focusing on the problem, not the personality, offers a degree of emotional detachment and avoids the blame game. There are also no benefits to waffling and trying to defuse a situation by relentless talking; instead, cover the facts and avoid passing judgement. Keeping it factual also means we are less likely to take things personally ourselves. But this requires us to prepare for difficult conversations – and in preparation we will find confidence.

4. **Reach conclusions**. To move forward positively, we need to find some sort of resolution. This is not about giving in to someone else's demands; we must find a balance that works for both of us. Either way, a degree of compromise will be necessary. Epictetus said, "Every event has two handles – one by which it can be carried and one by which it can't. If your brother does you wrong, don't grab it by his wronging, because this is the handle incapable of lifting it. Instead, use the other – that he is your brother, that you were raised together, and then you will have hold of the handle that carries."

Difficult colleagues

As in every organisation, there are people in schools who seem to be deliberately difficult. They have the capacity to make life challenging for all around them. There is little we can do to change this disposition in another individual – we only have control over our own reactions and feelings.

We can apply the lessons we learned on compassion in chapter 3. We are not privy to how another member of staff genuinely feels or is finding their experience in education. So, rather than allowing our frustration to build up, we should try to recognise that they are only human. Judging others for their behaviour is a waste of energy and will not help anyone to move forward.

That shouldn't, however, excuse behaviour that starts to affect us negatively. If that is the case, then we need to sensitively discuss this with the colleague, explaining the impact their behaviour is having on us. It is important to be aware of tone here: try to be as positive and constructive as possible and avoid making accusations. Again, preparation in advance is vital for these conversations. And if there is no resolution, we need to make our feelings clear to management and ensure there is some sort of follow-up.

We will always experience frustrations in our work with colleagues. There will be disagreements and conflicts – the passion we all have for our work dictates that. The important thing is to focus on our own capacity to remain resilient and calm: that is what will help to sustain us and keep us from becoming overwhelmed.

Serene summary

Conflict has the potential to make our work in schools uncomfortable and challenging. To manage conflict effectively, we must seek to resolve issues proactively and ensure that sustaining positive relationships is at the heart of our work.

8. LEARNING FROM MISTAKES

Anxious anecdote

As the class rampaged out of the door, a huge sigh of relief escaped from Darrol. To say the lesson had been a disaster would be the understatement of the year.

Period 5 on a Friday was not the place, he now knew, to try a collaborative activity for the first time with this class. The revolving group task had degenerated into a revolving group chat, with young people gleefully leaping from one off-task conversation to another.

As he surveyed the bomb site of a classroom, Darrol knew that Monday's lesson was going to involve something very quiet indeed.

When the English teacher Chris Curtis set up his blog, *Learning From My Mistakes*,[18] almost 10 years ago, he didn't expect it to be quite so successful. Now, with more than a million views and the publication of a superb book, *How to Teach English*, Chris is one of the most popular educational bloggers in the UK.

The introduction to his blog illustrates why his writing is so popular:

"Welcome to my blog. It is a 'warts and all' view of my teaching career. Hopefully, some of my thoughts will inspire you. Or, they will prevent you from making some of the mistakes I have made in the past."

His humility is refreshing. Far too often, in any career, we sweep our errors under the proverbial carpet and pretend that the "warts" don't exist. Our social media age almost demands that we project an image of cool perfection and triumphant success, yet neither is the reality for anyone.

Through his writing, Chris wants to reflect carefully on how we can improve and to recognise that mistakes are an essential part of being human. When I asked him how this philosophy had helped him in his own teaching career, he was very clear:

---

18   https://learningfrommymistakesenglish.blogspot.com

"When I started my English PGCE course, I was surprised by the confidence of many around me. I was a 'mature student' and everybody else was much younger and more confident than I was. Vividly, I recall a moment when one student professed, in a discussion, that they saw teaching as a short-term thing and that they planned to teach for a few years and then become a consultant. I was impressed and amazed by their gumption, but realised that all of that had been crushed out of me.

For two years previously, I had worked in a job where I was constantly belittled and made to work excessively hard, while my manager did no work at all and planned his weekend activities. He was of the thinking that leaders don't work, they just tell people what to do. As a result, all my confidence was sapped and leached out of me. I was made to feel worthless on a regular basis, until I told him I didn't want, or need, his job any more.

Becoming a teacher was a new career and direction for me. I started from a very humble position. My experience from my previous job told me I was far from the best at things, so I was ready to admit my mistakes or errors. I was ready to say when I didn't understand things. I was ready to ask for help, when I needed it.

Being a teacher is a tricky thing. You need confidence to stand before a group of teenagers, but you also need humility to learn from the processes and things that happen in the classroom. It is a balancing act between confidence and humility. At the centre of this are the mistakes we make and continue to make. I say we need more confidence in showing humility – that was the impetus for my blog. I wasn't hearing people talk about their mistakes. I wasn't hearing people describe the things that didn't work. I wasn't hearing about the failures in the classroom. Instead, all I was hearing about were the miraculous things that people did.

Teaching is a hard job, but it is even harder when people pretend it is something else. When they gloss over the mistakes, errors and problems; when they present it as magic. That is unrealistic and damaging. The mistakes are hidden in teaching. Therefore, every NQT makes the same mistakes, because nobody is bold enough to speak out about them. We've got to a point in education where 'mistakes' are seen as a personal flaw and not a process that needs refining or reflecting. We have personalised teaching to the extent where we can't tell the difference between teacher and teaching.

As a leader of my subject, I openly talk about my mistakes in lessons. How else can I get the people around me to reflect on what does and doesn't work? If I am honest, then they can be honest, too.

Learning from your mistakes is something we expect from students, yet we rarely model it to students in what we do."

Perfectionism

Learning to accept our mistakes is a vital part of developing resilience. Those who try to do everything perfectly and are terrified of failure will, of course, find themselves immobilised by their fear of getting things wrong. Their inner critic will dominate.

Ironically, this fear of failure can be strongest among those who have never experienced failure. Their identity is so bound up with being successful that any misstep is a terrifying prospect – one that might lead to a complete loss of resilience. Instead of living in this way that limits us and holds us back, we need to recognise that setbacks are a part of life and mistakes are there to learn from.

Failure can happen no matter how hard you try to prevent it – knowing this will give you a healthier perspective that allows you to learn from your mistakes without letting them devastate you. A mistake can be unpleasant, embarrassing and even costly, but the resilience you gain from your inevitable errors will help you to draw even more fulfilment from your successes. Barack Obama, when looking back over his tenure as US president, said, "I've screwed up. I've been in the barrel tumbling down Niagara Falls. And I emerged and I lived. And that's always such a liberating feeling."[19]

Owning your mistakes

There is nothing worse than trying to pretend to ourselves or others that a mistake is not our fault. In order to use the mistake as a learning opportunity, we have to be ruthlessly honest. Sometimes we need to hold up our hands and seek help to deal with the consequences of a mistake. Honesty is always the best policy, and others will have more, not less, respect for us if we admit the truth.

After accepting what has happened, we need to create the time and space to reflect on the experience and identify what can be learned. Talking through what has happened with someone we trust is a useful way to put our reaction into perspective and prevent us from feeling overwhelmed. From this point, we can start to work to make things better and move forward.

We all have weaknesses and areas where we need to improve – we are only human. Mistakes allow us to see our weaknesses clearly and can help us to formulate a plan for how to improve. In 1919, Walt Disney was fired from one of his first jobs for – oh, the irony – a lack of creativity. His later success tells us that he reframed this early failure and turned it into a positive.

---

19   www.pbs.org/newshour/nation/obama-first-presidential-podcast-u-s cured racism

Classroom setbacks

We have spent hours constructing a masterpiece lesson, one we are confident meets the needs of every child in the class and will help them to finally get to grips with that challenging concept. Yet the reality does not live up to expectations: behaviour is poor and the students are no closer to grasping the concept. How do we cope with our inevitable feelings of frustration, resentment and dissatisfaction?

The classroom is never going to be a good place for a perfectionist – there are too many variables and so many different elements that can influence a class dynamic, everything from the time of day to the strength of the wind! We need to recognise that the lesson will never be perfect and we will likely never reach the lofty heights we strive for. Keep in mind the experience of your training year: how often did you spend hours preparing something that ultimately just didn't work?

Experienced teachers will admit to cultivating a healthy degree of dispassion in their work. The issue with the scenario above is our level of emotional investment in the lesson, which is only to be expected after all the time and effort that went into constructing it. Experienced teachers are detached enough to apply a clinical level of honesty to their reflections on a poor lesson: what exactly went wrong? Internally castigating ourselves will not help the young people in front of us – we have to show the maturity to recognise our mistakes and work out how to stop them happening again.

Frustration can also come from the frequent battle of trying to encourage knowledge retention in our students. It is very easy to castigate the young people in front of us and become resentful of their inability to understand. A more resilient approach would be to give ourselves scope to reflect: we become empowered by looking at the different ways in which we could have explored the content. We can also keep reminding ourselves that even when things don't go so well, there are positives to be found. As Leonard Cohen sings in *Anthem*, "There is a crack in everything, that's how the light gets in."

Plan

Rachel Ball is an assistant principal in charge of teaching and learning at an academy in Salford. She has teaching for almost 19 years and this year set up a blog with another teacher called *The Educational Imposters*.[20] Rachel has kindly allowed me to reproduce here one of her first blog posts, entitled "How to fail as a teacher and leader". It is an excellent account of the importance of failure and of how Rachel has used failure positively to become more resilient. Reading it reminded me of this Chinese proverb: "A gem is not polished without rubbing, nor a person perfected without trials."

---

20   https://theeducationalimposters.wordpress.com

"Failure is something we all have in common. Whether it's failure to pass a driving test, to break the 25-minute barrier on a 5K run, to win a coveted award, to keep the house tidy, or whether it's more significant 'failures' around relationships, children, friendships or work, we all experience failure.

One of my first failures in teaching was the failure to get a job. As the rest of my cohort all seemed to manage to secure positions, I went to a few interviews where it seemed I did well, often getting down to the last two applicants before not being chosen for the position. My references were good, I was told my lessons were good and yet time ticked on, and before I knew it, it was July and I still had nothing for September. I think one of the issues was that my subject of history is a popular one and jobs were not as easy to come by as in some subjects, but at the time I felt an overwhelming sense of failure. I couldn't help but feel rejected, and it took me right back to never being picked for PE teams at school.

Interviews for me, as an introvert, are highly uncomfortable. I don't like having to sell myself, I forget my achievements and dwell on my failures, and spend hours afterwards analysing what I've said. Perhaps my shyness came across in interview, or perhaps I just wasn't a right fit for the schools I applied to. I will never know, but each and every one of those failed interviews taught me something, whether it was about lesson pitching, how much to attempt in a 20-minute lesson, experience of varied questions in interviews or just not to wear that particular skirt which digs in and makes you uncomfortable.

Ironically, when I eventually got a job in early July, I initially thought about not applying as the job was a 50% RE timetable and a temporary contract. I went along to the interview anyway, was honest and open and not as nervous as I had been in the others, and was offered the job straight away. Perhaps I had been trying too hard to fit in, perhaps I just found my groove, perhaps it was meant to be. Whatever the reason, I think I needed to experience that rejection before I got the job I did. It made me more appreciative of the responsibility I have as a teacher. It made me realise how important finding the right school for you is (when I look back, I don't think some of those schools would have been) and it made me more determined to prove myself.

My second failure was around relationships with pupils – something I think many, if not all, of us experience. My first year was extremely difficult. Of course, I started the year full of great intentions to make a difference, to inspire and to be the next LouAnne Johnson or Erin Gruwell. I ended up with a very apathetic Year 9 form class who had already been passed from pillar to post and thought of me as just another short-term stop gap. I also taught them history as a form group, along with a couple of other groups who did everything they could to try and break me, it seemed.

Lessons were an exhausting hour and 20 minutes and on Thursday mornings I taught the two most difficult classes back-to-back in a double. By Thursday lunchtimes most weeks, you could find me crying at my desk convinced I would never make it through the year. I regularly considered whether teaching was right for me. It didn't help that while I did have some support in the school, there were teachers who worked closely with me who did little to help, telling me I needed to toughen up and not spend so long on my lessons because 'they're not going to do it anyway'.

I think, looking back, I did toughen up – perhaps not in the way they expected. I raised my standards and kept them high. I stood my ground and worked on the little things like entrance to the lesson and routines for speaking in class. But more than that, I worked on relationships. I realised that these pupils needed to know I was invested in them, that I cared and that I believed in them. I spent time getting to know them, finding common ground and showing I had seen their potential. Relationships take time to develop and it was definitely not something that improved overnight. In fact, relationships are still something I need to work on even now, 19 years in.

But that initial year of seeming failure taught me so much about the kind of environment I wanted my classroom to be, the kind of teacher I wanted to be and the support I wanted to be for colleagues going through an experience like mine in the future. I'm proud to say that many of those pupils, some of them now parents themselves, have been in touch over the years and have thanked me for believing in them and challenging them, opening up about tough times they were going through. You see, it was never really about me. It wasn't personal – and that's the other lesson I've taken away from that incredibly difficult year.

I always set out to be the best teacher I could be, but it's only now, looking back, that I see another failure I had was in failing to understand how pupils actually learn, and therefore how best to teach them. To be fair, this probably was a failure of my training. Much as I enjoyed it, I don't remember ever being taught about memory or cognitive load, and therefore how could I best structure my lessons to ensure that pupils would learn in the most efficient and effective way?

Over the years my head was swayed by the latest fashion in teaching: poundland pedagogy, Kagan, thinking hats, competition, VAK and limiting teacher talk to no more than five minutes (I was once timed at an interview). I vividly remember teaching some lessons using playdough, where I doubt pupils learnt anything at all, and got sucked into wanting my observations to always be 'outstanding' – I remember crying once when I only got 'good' (obviously knowing now these gradings mean absolutely nothing).

And yet it's only over the past couple of years, when I have spent so much time investing in research and evidence-based practice, that I realise that much of what I had been doing was, at best, a waste of time and, at worst, overloading pupils' cognitive load and preventing actual learning from taking place. Reading, among others, Daniel Willingham's Why Don't Students Like School?, *Tom Sherrington's* The Learning Rainforest *and* Rosenshine's Principles in Action, *Matt Pinkett and Mark Roberts'* Boys Don't Try?, *Mary Myatt's* The Curriculum: Gallimaufry to Coherence, *Kate Jones'* Retrieval Practice, *Mark Enser's* Teach Like Nobody's Watching *and Chris Runeckles'* Making Every History Lesson Count *has utterly transformed my teaching. Teach to the top and scaffolding down; high challenge, low threat; frequent retrieval practice; direct instruction; a focus on challenging texts and scholarship in the classroom; and whole-class feedback have replaced the gimmicks of the past, which were only failing the pupils in front of me.*

Almost six years ago, my dad died aged just 69. I am the oldest of four and looked up to him immensely. He was the kindest man you could wish to meet. He had a big heart and would do anything for anyone, he loved to laugh and make mischief, and he could fix anything at all. He was fit, healthy and, having just retired from being a minister, seemed to have a happy retirement ahead of him. And yet, one day he visited the doctors complaining of nausea and just not being himself. The doctor took one look at him and sent him to A&E with jaundice, and he never really came home again, bar a brief weekend.

Twelve weeks later, he died in a hospice from tumours in his bile duct and liver which were inoperable, too weak for any chemotherapy or other intervention. It was a huge shock for me and my family, and my next failure relates to how I dealt with that grief, especially at work. I took the course of action of burying my feelings and throwing myself into work, going back far too soon and believing that, as head of a large faculty in school, to show how I was feeling would be a sign of weakness. I became hardened to the pain and didn't really talk about how I was feeling. In retrospect, I know those feelings had to come out at some time and they eventually did, when I lost it at school one day and could not stop sobbing.

It was my then headteacher who took me to one side that day and spoke to me at length about what I was going through. He asked me why I was pretending not to suffer, and challenged me about why I thought showing how I was feeling would make me a weaker leader. I'll always be grateful for that challenge. Since then I've read a lot about authentic leadership and how being aware of your emotions and being honest about your weaknesses can be a positive thing as a leader, often strengthening people's belief in you. Having gone through the experience of losing my dad, I hope that makes me a more empathetic and compassionate colleague and leader, but I also hope that next time I suffer in that way I'll know showing grief or pain is not a weakness – that it is not something you can repress or bury.

The last area of failure I have been reflecting on is my failure to have confidence and belief in my own capabilities, a topic I explored in my imposter syndrome blog post.[21] As I mention in the blog, it's hard to feel at times that you have something important to say, and in the world of teaching, particularly on Twitter, it's easy for your voice to get drowned out, or not to have the confidence to say anything at all.

This crippling fear has prevented me from going for promotion or new jobs at times and led to deep-rooted feelings of inadequacy. Comparison really is the thief of joy, and as I look back on my career so far, I wish I hadn't failed at times to see my strengths or been scared off by opportunities. As I've got older and learnt techniques to deal with my imposter syndrome, I've got stronger and more confident, more able to push myself beyond my comfort zone, and the results have been far more than I could have imagined.

Starting this blog with Katie is just one example. Sharing my imposter syndrome post and having so many people express similar feelings is a success borne out of failure, much as I hope this post will be, and takes us right back to where we started: failure is inclusive. I know failure will and does still happen to me and there are many more failures I could write about. I'm a leader and teacher who makes mistakes frequently, but it's important to acknowledge we all have those failures. I've learnt that failure can be turned into the greatest achievements, that mistakes can lead to the greatest growth.

*I write this post in the hope that even just one person feels less alone and that what I've talked about resonates, that it helps us become more connected. And I hope it shows that failure can be a force for good. I'll leave the final words to Elizabeth Day, without whose book [*How to Fail, Fourth Estate*] I would not have written this post: 'What does it mean to fail? I think all it means is that we're living life to its fullest. We're experiencing it in several dimensions, rather than simply contenting ourselves with the flatness of a single, consistent emotion. We are living in technicolour, not black and white.' I know I, for one, want to live in technicolour."*

---

21   https://theeducationalimposters.wordpress.com/2020/04/19/living-with-imposter-syndrome

Mistakes and difficulties, as Rachel's reflections show, leave us stronger and enrich our experiences. They come in many different guises and reflect the complexity of working in a school environment. There is so much potential for error in teaching and the reality is that we will make mistakes every day. What Rachel's blog post highlights, however, is that old-fashioned cliché that mistakes fuel our future and make us stronger. As Seneca says, "Difficulties strengthen the mind, as labour does the body."

In this section of the book we have explored the various facets of a calm and resilient mindset and how developing this mindset requires discipline and practice. The key is to maintain an open mind and to experiment with the strategies. In Part III, we will move on to practical actions that teachers can take to support and build their resilience. The first is very simple: sleep more.

Serene summary

Mistakes are a part of being human. You will inevitably make mistakes in the teaching profession, but by making a plan for how to learn from them and move forward, you can use your mistakes positively.

PART III: TEACHER ACTIONS

'Our greatest glory is not in never falling, but in rising every time we fall'
Confucius

9. SLEEP

Anxious anecdote

3.30am. Tara's eyes flick open and her mind clicks instantly into overdrive. "What will Billy be like in today's lesson? How will I complete that data analysis by the end of the day? What am I going to do about that huge pile of marking?"

3.45am. "Must go back to sleep. Must go back to sleep... Why can't I sleep?"

4.15am. "That's it: another day of utter exhaustion awaits. I can't go on like this for much longer..."

Sleep and teachers have an uneasy relationship. The compressed and intense nature of our jobs – with so much packed into short term times and days full of high-adrenaline activity – can make it hard for us to gain the seven or eight hours of sleep a night that is recommended for adults. We are notoriously busy and this can leave our minds permanently alert and full; there simply seems to be too much to do to make sleep a priority. Yet this is hugely problematic: sleep is the cornerstone of our health.

For those of us with an anxious temperament, sleep can be even more challenging. Our ruminations often strike at the most inconvenient of times and are hugely effective at preventing relaxation. The impact can be greatest when our heads first hit the pillow: like an alarm, this can trigger an avalanche of unwanted reflections and fretting. Or, alternatively, we might be prone to early-morning waking – this has always been my personal sleep demon. These difficulties with sleep can be a real indication of weakened resilience.

The hailing of the "teacher work ethic" can prove detrimental when it comes to conversations about sleep. There is always the "heroic" figure who will loudly outline how little sleep they have had because they have been up all night marking. This fetishises the sacrificing of sleep to meet work demands – something that ultimately makes us less effective and more prone to stress and anxiety.

Anyone who has had a bad night's sleep knows the impact on our brains – they can feel foggy and slow to react. In a profession that requires us to perform the best versions of ourselves, this is certainly not the way to start the day.

The importance of sleep

Even a cursory glance at Matthew Walker's book *Why We Sleep* is enough to raise serious concerns about the rejection of sleep in favour of catching up on work. His fundamental premise is that modern society's relationship with sleep is flawed: "Humans are not sleeping the way nature intended. The number of sleep bouts, the duration of sleep, and when sleep occurs has all been comprehensively distorted by modernity."

Even more alarming than this notion of sleep distortion is the link that Walker points out between lack of sleep and ill health:

> *"The shorter your sleep, the shorter your life. The leading causes of disease and death in developed nations – diseases that are crippling health-care systems, such as heart disease, obesity, dementia, diabetes, and cancer – all have recognized causal links to a lack of sleep."*

Walker's research connects sleep with resilience in two distinct ways:

1. **Good sleep is essential for learning**. Sleep allows us to acquire knowledge – our brains work to process new information for several nights after the initial learning.
2. **Sleep is essential for emotional regulation**. Brain scans of sleep-deprived people show increased activity in regions of the brain that generate reactivity and impulse, as well as decreased activity in regions that control rational decision-making. This is why a sleep-deprived person often swings between emotional extremes.

It is clear that we cannot expect to build our mental resilience without first addressing our sleep. Poor sleep will make us more susceptible to anxiety and stress. Conversely, more sleep will boost our wellbeing and enable us to live more healthy, committed, engaged and productive lives.

Before we look at strategies that will help us to prioritise sleep and make the most of the sleep time we have, it is important to highlight that sleep, much like aspects of our wellbeing, varies according to the individual. The reasons for this are complex – it can be dependent on your DNA or on the kind of personality you have. Experts also suggest that you should identify the factors that are most disruptive to your own sleep, then focus on altering particular behaviours and patterns to overcome these issues. We need, therefore, a differentiated approach to sleep, one that allows us to reflect on our own unique circumstances.

There are two main ways in which we can improve our relationship with sleep: the first involves building greater awareness of our behaviour throughout the day; the second is about sleep hygiene – how we prepare for sleep and the conditions in which we experience it. The rest of this chapter will illustrate some of the research-tested routes to better sleep.

Staying self-aware

Much of what we have already explored in this book has been about fostering greater self-awareness: recognising when we are feeling overwhelmed, and empowering ourselves with strategies that can help to alleviate stress and anxiety. Rather than being dictated to by outside forces, we need to decide how best we work and what helps to make teaching more manageable for us.

That individual ownership also has to be applied to sleep: we should not allow our sleep patterns to be dictated by other factors. Of course, there will inevitably be times when we are busier or more stretched. Or, like me, your sleep may be broken not by work demands but by young children!

That said, there is an ultimate truth about sleep: no matter how good our sleep hygiene is, if we are experiencing significant anxiety then we are not going to sleep well. This can start from the minute we wake up in the morning – if we instantly check our emails or social media then we are beginning the day in a stressful frame of mind.

Sleep is complex and nuanced, and lack of sleep can often be attributed to psychological challenges experienced during the day. There is a significant correlation, for example, between anxiety, depression and sleep. That relationship is reciprocal: sleep problems can cause anxiety, and anxiety can disrupt your sleep.

Our propensity for sleep problems caused by anxiety can depend on our temperaments. Some individuals have a wide emotional landscape that is sensitive to subtle influences. These individuals may process things more deeply, so at night their brains are more likely to churn over the events of the day. And let's be honest: teachers have a fairly wide and diverse range of things to reflect on!

Employing the strategies set out in the first section of the book, in terms of fostering more positive mindsets and taking practical steps to keep our work from overwhelming us, will lead to calmer days. This, in turn, will influence how well we are able to switch off at bedtime.

Winding down

Our minds need time to wind down and prepare for sleep. Working until the small hours and then stumbling into bed is clearly not conducive to a good night's sleep. Our brains need a chance to first become less active.

We need a point beyond which all work stops and we allow ourselves to do something else. This will vary for individuals, but I know that if I do anything work-related after 9pm, I will struggle to go to sleep. Or, because of the active nature of my brain when I go to sleep, I will wake up early in the morning.

Imposing a stopping point requires discipline and a little reflection on efficacy. Working into the small hours will not make you more effective; rather, it will have a detrimental impact on your energy levels and teaching the next day.

Step away from the screens

That self-imposed stopping point should also apply to our screens. As we will examine in greater detail in chapter 12, our lives are now deeply interconnected with our electronic devices and this can disrupt our sleep rhythms.

The main problem when it comes to electronic devices and sleep is that they keep our minds very alert. After half an hour of social media scrolling, we can feel wired and full of information. That makes it much more challenging for us to switch off and relax, which in turn has an impact on our sleep. And when your social media networks revolve around your work in education, it can be even more difficult to switch off.

Make your bedroom a sanctuary

Instead of being enslaved to our devices, we need to make our sleep environments as calm and technology-free as possible. Temperature is very important: the ideal bedroom temperature is around 18C; a room that's too warm or too cool can disrupt our sleep. Even the mattress can have a negative impact: we need to make sure it is not too hard and not too soft.

Lighting is also important. Soft lighting contributes to a calm and restful atmosphere, while the blue light emitted by screens can delay the release of sleep-inducing melatonin. Another reason to banish devices at bedtime!

A consistent routine

In my own struggles with sleep, the change that has been most effective has been going to bed and waking up at roughly the same time each day. I always get up at 6am so I can snatch a few moments of peace before my son wakes.

Parents are all too aware that children's sleep requires stringent management and a predictable routine. But routine is not just for children – it can also be very helpful for adults. Your body clock starts to get used to the routine you have set, and you begin to automatically slow down as bedtime approaches. You become "programmed" to fall asleep and wake up at a particular time. Some people go to great lengths to maintain their routine, even setting an alarm to remind them to go to bed.

Caffeine and exercise

Caffeine stays in our system for a surprisingly long time and can have a hugely detrimental impact on the quality of our sleep, as well as how we respond to stress during the day. Avoiding caffeine after 3pm (remember it can be found in chocolate as well as tea, coffee, cola and energy drinks) and limiting consumption before then will mean it is out of your system by the evening. Doing some form of exercise for 30 minutes a day, but not too close to bedtime, will also aid your sleep.

When you can't sleep

The following steps are to be employed when you are finding it difficult to get to sleep.

1. **Meditate**. A deputy headteacher I worked with told me that if he couldn't sleep, he would get up and spend half an hour meditating to try to calm his mind. He would usually find that he could get to sleep afterwards. Often, it is the feeling of panic that keeps us awake, but even 10 minutes of trying to focus on your breath can calm a frantic mind and provide some sense of perspective. In *Why We Sleep*, Walker writes: "When I was researching the book, I dived right in to the world of science so the idea of meditation seemed a bit woo-woo to me. But the data is incredibly compelling so I started meditating myself. It's a wonderfully efficacious tool to help just calm the brain and the body down. That's normally what keeps people awake at night. They wake up and anxiety starts going through their mind."
2. **Don't lie in bed awake**. If you find yourself lying in bed for longer periods of time, getting up and doing something else might keep you from becoming embroiled in the internal mind wars. Reading a book for 20 minutes or finding a place to meditate might help you to relax and switch off.
3. **Avoid catastrophising**. In the deep of the night, every stress and anxiety is magnified to take on terrifying proportions. As we explored earlier, detaching from the thoughts and recognising that they are disproportionate will keep us from becoming caught up in them.

Managing a tired day

Inevitably, there will be nights when we don't sleep well, no matter how closely we adhere to a sleep schedule or how stringent our sleep hygiene. The feeling of dread that accompanies a night of broken sleep can have a huge impact on the following day. So, how can we cope on a tired day?

1. **Remember self-compassion**. If we are tired, we are not going to teach and act at our very best – we don't have the reserves to do that. So, we need to go slow and be more patient with ourselves. An internal voice of care and understanding will be much more beneficial than a critical one.
2. **Plan accordingly**. Being proactive and managing the day carefully will prevent exhaustion from becoming overwhelming. That means not filling the day with teacher-led activities and talk, and instead going for balance. A period of well-managed collaborative learning, or longer periods of silence in which young people work individually, will help us to sustain our energy.
3. **Be open**. There is no point in bottling everything up – it only makes the situation worse. Being open and sharing with colleagues any sleep issues you might be experiencing can lighten the strain. They might help you to see beyond your anxiety about sleep and spot some solutions.

If there is one message to take from this chapter, it is this: prioritise your sleep. Sleep is more important than any piece of marking, any email or any piece of work that you are struggling to finish. For teachers, restorative sleep is vital to allow us to perform at our best.

Serene summary

To ensure a good night's sleep, we need self-awareness and sleep hygiene. We must recognise the importance of sleep, and reflect on the stress and anxiety we experience during the school day. Setting clear sleep routines, rationing screen time, stopping work at a reasonable hour and avoiding caffeine will positively affect how well we sleep at night.

10. SETTING BOUNDARIES

Anxious anecdote

With her usual brisk efficiency, the head of department swung her head round the door. "John, I'm looking for some volunteers to help with the sixth-form open evening. Can I put your name down? You're always so keen to get involved."

John hesitated. "Er...I've got a lot of marking on at the moment."

"Don't worry, it's only for a few hours. I would be so grateful." There was an expectant pause. Finally, John gave in.

"OK. No problem."

His tired smile masked the internal torment: why can't I just say no? Why do I always end up being the one who does these things?

For teachers, trying to juggle the extensive demands is clearly a major factor in feelings of stress and anxiety. Yet we often put ourselves forward to do things that will only compound the problem. One thing that many teachers struggle with is setting and maintaining boundaries.

Learning to say no is integral to building a more resilient mindset. It gives us the ability to control our time and dictate our own ways of working. Its alternative – saying yes to everything – is clearly unhealthy, resulting in a treadmill-like existence where we are frantically busy at all times.

We all want to be perceived as helpful and there for others. Some schools exploit the goodwill of teachers, their natural wish to please and their reflex to obey authority structures. Teachers may also have a desire to control that can make it hard to give up responsibility or delegate – we want to be in charge of our own classes and environments. Indeed, learning to understand our inclination to always say yes is an important part of developing the capacity to say no. It helps us to recognise our own behaviour patterns.

In my first five years of teaching I had absolutely no boundaries. I taught in a school where early promotion was common and a culture of long hours and utter commitment was normalised. I was also ambitious: I wanted to be promoted and I wanted to have the opportunity to make a difference.

To achieve that I worked relentlessly, arriving at school at 6am, leaving at 7pm and then working deep into the evenings at home. There was no cut-off point. And I added more and more to my plate by nodding enthusiastically at everything that was thrown my way. As a classroom teacher I just about got by, but when I did receive the promotion to senior management that I had strived for, I worked longer and harder until my body couldn't cope any more. As you read in chapter 4, I eventually had a breakdown.

It has taken me some time to learn from these mistakes and develop a much deeper sense of self-awareness. I now understand that to thrive in our demanding profession, we have to be our own gatekeepers. We have to be robust and assertive in controlling our time. We need to follow the example of Oliver Sacks, who hung a sign in his office that read "No!" to remind him not to overcommit.

Better boundaries

Boundaries are so important in ensuring that you have control of your own working pattern. That pattern needs to be realistic and manageable. As an NQT, I set a pattern of being in school from 7am until 7pm, inspired by a comment made by the headteacher in one of our first meetings that implied this was a good pattern to follow.

I was young and earnest. I stretched this pattern consistently until, as I mentioned earlier, I was arriving at 6am. I was completely absorbed by the culture and had lost sight of the necessity of work-life balance. This practice, exploited by some schools, is common among new teachers. As one teacher told the charity Education Support, "I had completely lost my boundaries, I didn't know where my job ended and myself started. It had all become this glutinous, amorphous thing."[22]

As teaching is a job where such practices are culturally acceptable, we need to impose our own limits on how much we do. Those limits will vary according to our individual circumstances. Since becoming a father, I have had to become so much better at setting boundaries and I am still learning about how best to do this. My wife now has a job with much more responsibility and longer hours than me, which means I need to be absolutely regimented about my working pattern to make sure that our childcare arrangements work.

If we are more disciplined about how we use our time, we start to think more strategically and embrace long-term planning. The better we get at this, the easier our job becomes. The key point is that your work-life balance is dictated by *you* and you need to carefully plan how you will achieve it. Balance will not happen by osmosis.

---

22   www.educationsupport.org.uk/grappling-work-life-balance

We will always become more efficient as we gain more experience, but it can be helpful to seek advice from those around us. How do teachers who are further along in their careers manage their time? Is there a teacher in your department who manages their time efficiently and effectively? What are their tips?

Of course, how work-life balance is achieved will depend on the individual, but here are a couple of things that have helped me and worked for others:

1. **Separate school and home**. Your circumstances might not allow for this, but it is very hard to maintain a healthy separation when we bring work home with us every evening. Is it possible to complete work in school rather than take it home? This might not happen every day, but having some self-imposed evenings away from work will make life more manageable. If work has to be taken home, leaving it a different room can create a bit of distance. A gigantic pile of books lurking in the corner of the living room is not conducive to relaxation! I have always been fortunate to live close enough to school that I can run home – an apt metaphor for escaping the stresses and strains of the day! This journey marks a clear transition from school to home and helps to make the boundaries clearer. Others might spend some time reflecting when they get home or go out for a walk – anything that helps them to switch off.
2. **Take breaks.** It is not healthy to remain on the teacher treadmill for the entire day. Sometimes you need to force yourself to take a break. You might take 10 minutes for a cup of coffee, or go up to the staffroom for lunch and a debrief with colleagues. Choose what works best for you. You might prefer to sit quietly and individually for a period of time, or go for a walk around the block.

Assertive communication

To take control over our working habits, it helps to embrace a more assertive mode of communication. Saying no is a significant part of that and the chances are that it will make you more, not less, respected.

The Anxious Anecdote that opened this chapter illustrates the desire to please that can be common among teachers. We fear the prospect of letting people down and failing to pull our weight. But saying no is perhaps more essential in teaching than in any other profession. With all the demands we face, learning to say no is vital to preserve our health and prevent us from being overwhelmed by stress.

A good approach is to be proactive in seeking out the additional projects or events that you *want* to be involved with. For me, this has always involved sharing my passions by trying to set up running or writing clubs in school.

Before we agree to do additional things, we need to reflect on the benefits for us. That may sound selfish, but it is an appropriate degree of selfishness, since we are being asked to do something that will demand more from us and may eat into our life outside school. Always ask for time to consider before committing to a task. Think carefully about the task and why it would matter to you. Another useful perspective to take is: will you look back in the future and be glad that you did it?

If you decide to say no, always express this politely and clearly, and be honest about your reasons. It can be helpful to first express a degree of gratitude for being asked to do something, before going on to highlight why it might not be possible. Recommending others or trying to delegate tasks ensures that your refusal is delivered in a positive way.

Since writing *A Quiet Education*, about introverts in schools, and openly admitting my preference for solitude, saying no has become much easier for me – particularly when it comes to social events! Here are some alternatives to yes:

- "I appreciate being asked, but I'm afraid I have too much on at the moment."
- "Thank you for considering me for this, but I'm sorry, I'm not available to help."
- "That sounds great, but I would rather not."
- "I'm sorry, I can't commit to this because…"

It is important that you are not persuaded against your first answer – be firm and polite in repeating why you cannot commit to something. And don't let yourself feel any guilt for your refusal – it is absolutely right and proper that you stick to your boundaries.

A phrase that has worked particularly well for me is "I have a rule". People tend to understand and respect the idea that we set rules for ourselves, and that can help us to gently say no to something that comes up. One of my rules relates to being able to pick up my son from childcare: "I have a rule that I am back in time to pick up my wee boy." Another relates to technology: "I have a rule that I take two months away from social media every year, and that I don't send emails at the weekend."

Open and honest
The more we accept the things that pile pressure on teachers, the more teachers will burn out and leave the profession. Sometimes, we have to have the courage to push back and say no. We need to be open, setting out exactly how much time we are spending on things and the consequences of that. This can often be

revealing and shocking – and it can help to realign the balance. At the start of a career this can be difficult to do, but with time and experience we can learn to say no.

The conversation around setting professional boundaries and sticking to them might not be ubiquitous in the teaching profession, but I would argue that it is one of the most important discussions we can have. Of course, there is a balance to be found, and part of being a teacher is engaging in the broader school community in the ways that work best for you. The key, however, is keeping control over what you engage in.

Serene summary

In order to maintain a healthy work-life balance, and to provide our pupils with the best we can, we need to set boundaries. Those boundaries should dictate our working habits and what we do in the school environment. We must also be assertive and clear in our communication. In doing so, we can feel comfortable in how we are approaching our work and confident that we are making it as manageable as possible.

11. LESSON OBSERVATIONS

Anxious anecdote

Friday morning, 7.55am. Jess sits down at her desk and begins as she usually does, wading through the flood of emails. Anxiety hits as she moves the mouse towards a new email with the title "Progress scrutiny" from the deputy headteacher:

"Your class has been chosen as part of senior management's progress scrutiny. You will be observed for 30 minutes on Monday. Please make sure a detailed lesson plan, seating plan and current data information regarding progress is available. We will be looking at the progress of pupil premium students, attainment levels, enthusiasm for learning and behaviour."

Jess's mind instantly starts to whirr: "Pupil premium students, attainment levels, behaviour, enthusiasm – all in 30 minutes? How on earth am I going to demonstrate that? Billy is guaranteed to be a nightmare, and Monday period 5 is their worst lesson of the week. And what do they mean by 'current data information regarding progress'?

"Well, that's the weekend completely ruined."

There are very few teachers who are not struck by some degree of anxiety when told they are going to be observed – or, as in Jess's case, "scrutinised". Anything that involves judgement can set off our fight or flight response as we consider the dangers and the threats.

The stress is compounded by the three facets of an observation: the fretting beforehand, the adrenaline of the lesson itself and the discussion afterwards. What could be a useful and empowering professional experience designed to improve what we offer young people in the classroom is reduced to one associated only with anxiety and stress.

The language surrounding observations leads to further negative associations. In the email received by Jess, the term "progress scrutiny" implies a critical examination – a search for deficits. "Performance management" is another common term, one that suggests the performance of a fellow professional needs to be managed; this can alienate them from their ability to reflect on their own performance. Neither term implies a collegiate conversation or a dialogue focused on growth or improvement. Neither appears to consider the emotional impact on schools' most valuable commodity: their teachers.

The fact that someone is entering our classroom ostensibly to make a judgement on our teaching adds another layer of stress to the act of standing up in front of 30 young people. The power dynamic has a significant influence on us, but also on how the students respond to our teaching during the lesson.

The run-up to an observation often involves obsessive planning, overthinking and doubt. If the observation is introduced through an impersonal email, such as the one received by Jess, this can fuel fear about the consequences of a poor outcome. There is no relationship, no easing of the pressure, no awareness of the anxiety that receiving this on a Friday might cause over the weekend.

Of course, Jess's story is fictional, but I have been on the receiving end of such outlines of expected content and I know how common such practices are. Any management team should know that it is impossible to measure all those aspects in a 30-minute period. Ultimately, this can only lead to a tick-box observation process, rather than any meaningful pedagogical feedback. An observation culture like this will only deepen distrust and reduce professional autonomy, creating the sense that teaching and learning in this context is something *done* to teachers, rather than something that is discussed and explored collaboratively.

The problem with observations

Some school systems make lesson observations very challenging for staff to approach positively. In a dystopian, Orwellian culture of micro-management, observations are conducted by leaders merely to exert control over teachers. It would be naive to think that the grading system that characterised my own training is not still being employed by some schools.

The fact that our teaching can be reduced to a summative grade adds even more anxiety to the observation process. I used to pore over the Ofsted "outstanding" framework and cynically design observed lessons to match each criteria. I'm embarrassed to admit that this often mattered more to me as an NQT than whether my students learned something substantial.

For my first ever observation as an NQT, I was graded "outstanding" by management, which illustrates just how nonsensical the grading system is. I was not, and still am not, anywhere near the level that the word "outstanding" suggests. All that was required from me was a performance that fitted a criteria for a lesson – and this is a superficial and reductive way to examine teaching.

"Outstanding" has its roots in perfection and I would argue that no lesson, or teaching, ever reaches perfection. I prefer now to consider my teaching with the words of Socrates in mind: "The only true wisdom is in knowing you know nothing." Adopting an open and expansive mindset, one that is always developing, is far less anxiety-inducing than aiming for perfection and always leaves room for the improvements that can inevitably be made.

Sometimes, the people who give lesson feedback have interpersonal skills that appear to have been lost somewhere in translation. The post-observation discussion becomes a didactic account of what was wrong with the lesson – an exercise in power rather than meaningful feedback. We will look at how to manage these situations as the chapter progresses.

There is still much we can do on an individual level to prevent lesson observations from keeping us awake at night. First, we need to be aware of some of the cognitive traps we can fall into when we find out we are going to be observed.

Controlling the uncontrollable

Anxiety makes us want to control things – to reduce the risk of failure and make sure everything is perfect. With lesson observations, that tendency can become hugely exaggerated. I carefully prepared for my NQT observations, spending hours poring over every detail to ensure there was no area in which I could stumble. This spoke not of confidence in my ability as a teacher, but of a deep-rooted fear of being caught out. Any sensible observer, upon receiving a pages-long lesson plan overview, would have tried to guide me away from such thinking and suggested that my time would be much better spent elsewhere. I was trying to control the uncontrollable.

The result of this endless thought loop, which plays the different aspects of the observation over and over, is that the pressure on the "judgement" becomes even more intense. By the time the lesson arrives, we are so exhausted and so full of adrenaline and anxiety that it becomes a hugely stressful experience.

Remember that it is easy to become lost in paperwork as a teacher: to write out reams of information for every lesson observation and every child. Do only what is required of you by the school – that time and energy could be better used elsewhere.

Putting on a show

We want to showcase our best teaching to an observer – that is only natural. When the observation finally arrives, however, the lesson itself is a million miles from the reality of our everyday practice. It packed full of collaborative activities and driven at a manic pace.

This has an unsettling effect on us and on the young people: we are acting in a way that is not our natural teaching style. I am not arguing that we should not invest time and thought into planning a strong lesson for an observation, but it has to be authentic. And if we remain authentic, any feedback we receive will help us to move forward with our practice.

Expecting perfection

What drives this need for validation from an external other? The fact that some schools facilitate very little in the way of frequent lesson feedback heightens the expectations surrounding one lesson observation.

We often receive very little informed and direct feedback – the moans of an adolescent about a "boring" lesson are sometimes the most feedback we hear for weeks on end. Thus, our self-efficacy and self-esteem can be more fragile than in other professions.

Instead of seeing lesson observations as delivering an almighty judgement on us as practitioners, it is useful to reframe them as opportunities to learn. No matter how much experience we have in our classrooms, a fresh pair of eyes and a new perspective can help to improve the quality of our lessons.

We need to see lesson feedback not as a personal slight, but as a way to make us even better. That is why it is important that we present the reality of our classroom on a daily basis and don't feel pressure to put on some kind of show for the observation.

There must be a school-wide policy that staff *always* receive feedback after an observation. When someone comes into our classroom and leaves no feedback, it achieves nothing good. It creates a gulf between us and the observer, it feeds internal anxiety about not being good enough, and it fails to lead to improvement or clarity about the kind of practice the observer was looking for.

Reflect and lead

We have all received shockingly bad lesson feedback in our time. Some people are more gifted at delivering feedback than others. Taking ownership of the experience and getting in early with your own reflections about the lesson can help to guide the discussion in a positive direction. In a conversation for my podcast,[23] Bruce Robertson, author of *The Teaching Delusion*, told me that his school approached lesson observations through a lesson evaluation toolkit:

> *"The key purpose of a school lesson evaluation toolkit is to direct the attention of teachers and school leaders to features of a lesson which*

---

23   https://tinyurl.com/y5dcv7kg

typically combine to produce high-quality teaching. It highlights,
summarises and signposts. It is not to tell teachers how they must teach.
Rather, it invites teachers to think about particular aspects of teaching
practice; for example, as they plan lessons, when they self-evaluate after
teaching or when they are discussing lessons with other members of staff.
It is the pivotal role of the lesson evaluation toolkit in self-evaluation
which has led to its name."

This idea is an empowering one that can help to ensure that any feedback is a discussion, rather than someone merely telling someone else how to teach. Such a process serves only to demotivate, de-intellectualise and generate more stress. But a lesson evaluation toolkit supports us to do what all good teachers do: continually reflect on what makes our lessons effective and what we need to do to improve.

If we can take a role in a feedback *conversation*, observation becomes less of a cause for anxiety. Rather than fixating on any overall judgment, we can see our work in the classroom as a skill that we are always reflecting upon and refining. This can support our development of resilience.

Maintain perspective

We will, at one time or another, receive lesson feedback that we disagree with. Some feedback is subjective and some observers are people who can't actually teach very well themselves! But the reality is that you are in a position where you need to accept the feedback. Arguing against lesson feedback is never very gracious or, indeed, successful. Questioning the observer will help to make sure the feedback we receive is precise and provides ideas and strategies for how to improve our teaching practice.

One reason why more formal lesson observations induce such fear is because we don't often have other people in our classrooms. But the more open we are about our classroom practice, the more natural the feedback process feels. Encouraging fellow teachers to pop in to a lesson for 10 minutes, to share some feedback on something new that we are trying, can help us to feel more confident about sharing our practice. It also provides motivation: we recognise that we are not perfect, but always learning.

There is something refreshing and healthy about accepting the fact that we will never be the perfect teacher, but that we will continue to grow and develop. Teaching can be a lonely experience, so the more we share with those around us, the more we will understand what makes good learning experiences for our students.

Find a coach

Finding a coach strips away the power dynamic that can influence managerial observations, instead allowing us to have real, honest dialogue about our teaching. Establishing a reciprocal coaching relationship with a colleague, in which you also visit their lessons and discuss their teaching, can be a powerful way to learn about effective dialogue in teaching and learning.

The next time someone tells you that your class is being observed, remember to breath, pause and recognise this as an opportunity to learn. In doing so, that observation can be viewed as a positive thing, rather than something to dread.

Serene summary

Lesson observations are one of the most anxiety-inducing aspects of teaching. But it doesn't have to be this way. We can reframe our thinking about observations and view them as positive opportunities for growth. Teaching is so multifaceted and complex that we will never master it. By refusing to put on a lesson "performance" and instead allowing observers an authentic insight into our daily practice, we can deepen our understanding of how to improve. Being open, responsive and proactive in the feedback process can also help to make it less stressful. As teachers, we encourage our students to learn wholeheartedly from their mistakes – this mindset will serve us well in our own growth and improvement.

12. BECOMING A DIGITAL MINIMALIST

Anxious anecdote

9.30pm. "Must get marking done. Must get marking done." But Desmond's finger twitched in the direction of the computer keyboard. He could hear the siren call of Facebook...

9.55pm. Desmond blinked and cast a blurry eye at the clock. Twenty-five minutes had suddenly evaporated. His new-found knowledge that Matilda, a long-lost friend from university, had a new puppy hadn't helped much with the marking.

He felt a growing dread as the long night stretched out before him: "How on earth am I going to get everything done in time?"

Confession: I would describe myself as a technological Luddite. I don't have a Facebook account and I have a slightly irrational fear of iPads. My lessons, to the dismay of my students, are pretty much free of technology. I have an old phone with no apps or email on it, and I avoid using its internet function.

I do use Twitter, because it has enabled me professionally and I have learned so much from it. I'm very aware that I wouldn't have received the opportunity to write these words if I hadn't joined Twitter. For me, it is clear that the benefits of this investment with technology outweigh the negatives.

I have, however, worked hard to make sure that I use Twitter in a way that I dictate, rather than being sucked into it more than is helpful or, indeed, healthy. I take two months away from Twitter every summer – most of the school holidays – and at least two days away from it every week.

I also drive my wife to despair by enforcing Screen-Free Sunday: a day that is completely free of screen-based technology. That means no TV, no laptops and no phones. Unsurprisingly, Sunday is the day of the week when I feel at my most calm and present. Going screen-free even helps to alleviate that Sunday night back-to-school anxiety – something that would once have left me feeling very on edge.

My rationale for embracing the principles of digital minimalism is very simple: when I overuse technology, I feel more anxious and wired. I also recognise the addictive and invasive nature of lots of social media and technology.

Such an approach, of course, isn't for everyone, but it makes sense to be thoughtful about the impact of technology on our levels of productivity and wellbeing. This requires us to be conscious and intentional about how we use technology.

Distraction sickness

I am very aware that technology is a tool that can enrich our lives and make us more efficient. Ostensibly, it should enable us to have much more time. Yet the never-ending nature of the information that arrives through our screens means that we are more absorbed in content and face more distractions than ever before.

An essay by Andrew Sullivan in *New York* magazine, entitled "I used to be a human being",[24] illustrates the insidiousness of technology. Writing about what he calls "distraction sickness", Sullivan says: "An endless bombardment of news and gossip and images has rendered us manic information addicts. It broke me. It might break you, too."

A significant amount of the distraction is novelty-based; it offers no real meaning or value. Cutting back can help with all aspects of our wellbeing and our capacity to be resilient. Given how much time pressure we are under as teachers, controlling our use of technology can also free up some time for meaningful activities outside of work.

Digital minimalism

Minimalism is something I have written about before: the notion of pruning back our lives to what is essential, and in doing so becoming more serene and more present. In my first book, *Slow Teaching*, I argued that applying the principles of minimalism to our classrooms could help us to feel calmer in our teaching. Joshua Fields Millburn and Ryan Nicodemus, the self-described Minimalists, define the movement as the following:

> *"Minimalism is a lifestyle that helps people question what things add value to their lives. By clearing the clutter from life's path, we can all make room for the most important aspects of life: health, relationships, passion, growth, and contribution."*[25]

24   https://nymag.com/intelligencer/2016/09/andrew-sullivan-my-distraction-sickness-and-yours.html
25   www.theminimalists.com/pitch

When applied to the digital world, the premise is simple. Cal Newport, the author of *Digital Minimalism*, summarises it as the following: "A philosophy of technology use in which you focus your online time on a small number of carefully selected and optimized activities that strongly support things you value, and then happily miss out on everything else." He recognises, however, that this drive to simplify and break free from superfluousness is not revolutionary, but deeply rooted in philosophical traditions.

Newport's book is persuasive. It gives readers examples of what can happen when we refuse to be ruled by technology, with calmer, more aware and more focused individuals the frequent result. He writes:

> "*This idea is not new. Long before Henry David Thoreau exclaimed 'simplicity, simplicity, simplicity,' Marcus Aurelius asked: 'You see how few things you have to do to live a satisfying and reverent life?' Digital minimalism simply adapts this classical insight to the role of technology in our modern lives.*"

The tyranny of email

My first school had an almost blanket ban on emails – there was really no whole-school way of sending emails. There was also a implicit understanding that you would never send or receive an email during the working day, because this would only serve as a distraction from the core purpose of being in school: teaching and learning.

I didn't fully appreciate the positives of this approach until I moved to a school where email was entirely unmanaged. Emails flooded in at all times of the day – early mornings, during teaching hours – and responses were expected. I found that I was much more distracted: my focus and concentration were broken every few minutes. Even worse was the fact that I was using my own computer in the evenings to try to keep the emails under control, so there was never a switch-off point.

Teachers are busy and often rushed, so the tone of the emails we receive can be more curt than intended, which sometimes generates anxiety and upset. Even something as innocuous as "Can we meet for a conversation at the end of the day?" can trigger uneasy fretting.

In a professional environment, face-to-face interactions are much more wholesome than emails and help to foster positive relationships. Combined with a structured and disciplined approach to managing email, they can make our school experience more positive.

Digitally minimalist email

After realising how much time his smartphone was consuming, the deputy headteacher Aidan Severs, who runs the blog *That Boy Can Teach*,[26] decided to ditch it for a month. As he wrote in an article for *Tes*,[27] "The smartphone exacerbates the situation. We are now constantly on call. We always have a catalyst to think about work because we know that in our pocket lies a tool that will potentially help us complete any outstanding tasks, allay any fears or confirm something with a colleague."

But rather than just ditching it for a month, Aidan has now been smartphone-free for a year. He sent me his reflections on how this has changed his life (and you can also hear him talk about his experience on my podcast[28]):

> "I became a digital minimalist before I'd even heard the term. I am an all-or-nothing kind of person and, after trying 101 other tricks to wean myself off my phone, I went for it: I bought a dumbphone for a few pounds, stuck my SIM card in and all of a sudden I was free.
>
> Free of the endless checking of social media and of the hours of idleness as I 'just checked' one thing after another. Free to interact with those around me in a way that deleting apps, turning off notifications and setting my smartphone to start up and shut off at allotted times just didn't allow. Free to read more, make more music and write more. Free to relax without the fast-paced world of the internet forcing my brain to run at speeds it was just not designed for.
>
> I've now been smartphone-free for over a year and that is my main claim to the title of 'digital minimalist'. I still use computers for work, for checking social media and emails, and for completing other life admin – it would be near impossible to live in today's world without doing so. But having to deliberately get out a laptop or boot up a computer means that my interactions with technology are much more deliberate and much less incidental.
>
> Going smartphone-free, I can confidently report, has removed a great deal of stress from my life and given me time for more worthwhile pursuits. For anyone considering doing the same, I can honestly say that I do not miss having a smartphone. Their negatives far outweighed the positives for me and I was able to replace the most important functions with less distracting things, such as a camera, a road atlas, a Spotify music player and a Garmin device. Plus, I now spend about £6 a month instead of the inordinate sums of money needed to stay up-to-date in the tech market."

26   www.thatboycanteach.co.uk
27   www.tes.com/magazine/article/could-you-survive-without-your-phone
28   www.slowteaching.co.uk/2020/05/11/take-control-work-life-balance

If ditching your smartphone seems like a step too far, there is another solution: don't have work emails on your phone. Another approach is to only respond to work emails at specific times of the day. Rather than being a slave to your emails and allowing yourself to be distracted as the notifications pop up on your phone, you could decide to check your emails first thing in the morning, then at lunchtime and once more at the end of the day.

It is really important to refuse to engage with emails in the evenings or outside school. This allows us to leave our work behind physically and mentally. Having school emails on our phones means that we are never really off-duty – something that strikes me as a recipe for greater stress and anxiety.

When *Tes* interviewed the headteacher Simon Smith about his school's email policy, he said: "We decided our times by sitting down with all of the staff to agree what was reasonable. Then, together, we came up with our parameters for when it is acceptable to send. If there is a safeguarding emergency, staff know that I might call, but otherwise, no emails outside of hours."[29]

During the Covid-19 lockdown, so much of our work was done through computers that it became even more important to have a switch-off point. As Aidan wrote in his *Tes* article,[30] "In some schools, there is a culture where teachers are expected always to respond to emails immediately, and always to be ready to chat about the next day's staffing issues on WhatsApp. Going smartphone-free in such a context could be a brave and potentially perilous thing to do. I am lucky my school is not like that."

When it comes to parental emails, I tend to respond with a request for a phone conversation with the parent. This is usually a timesaver: we can talk through the issues more quickly and with more nuance than in an email conversation.

Social media

Social media for teachers has grown rapidly over the past few years. The explosion of teacher blogs has been hugely empowering and provided insights not only into how different schools function, but also into what actually happens in other teachers' classrooms. Its collaborative potential is significant, serving to both inspire and engage.

Well-known educators are amassing hundreds of thousands of followers on Twitter; Ross Morrison McGill is one of the most popular, with almost 240,000 followers. His blog, www.teachertoolkit.co.uk, was founded in 2008 and now has more than 10 million readers. In 2015, Ross was named one of *The Sunday Times'* 500 Most Influential People in Britain.

---

29   www.tes.com/for-schools/blog/article/six-ways-banish-email-anxiety
30   www.tes.com/magazine/article/could-you-survive-without-your-phone

Although social media's positive impact cannot be denied, as with any technological tool there are, of course, negatives. The most obvious is the demands that it can make on our time. In 2017, Ross wrote on his website:

> *"In terms of managing my mental health, I have learnt how to switch off from school and from social media; to blog quicker and much less. With help from a small group of team members and a selection of teacher-bloggers who contribute, managing the two has become less of a burden for me. Of course I still tweet from @TeacherToolkit, but this blog over the past 12 months has taken on its own course – which has thankfully allowed me to spend more time with my family and still use the platform to support teachers across the world."*

A few clear negatives arise from overuse of social media, particularly education-focused social media:

1. **No off switch.** Balance, as I have learned the hard way, is necessary to flourish and live a happy life. An all-consuming focus on one thing can leave us vulnerable to mental health problems. Teachers, I have found, often face this issue. We spend a huge amount of our free time on social media sites, finding ourselves more and more immersed in education; we are defined by our profession.
2. **Addictive.** In his book, Newport argues that social media companies are "attention-economy conglomerates" whose aim is to grab your attention and sell it to advertisers. Social media sites are designed to be ruthlessly addictive, to entice us into spending longer on them than we might want to and to check them more often than is healthy.
3. **Feelings of inadequacy.** The temptation is to project an image of teaching perfection: to share pictures of lovingly curated displays, or to write blog posts about profound impacts that have been made in the classroom. But, rather than energising teachers, this can make us feel rather dejected about our own classrooms and abilities. As Theodore Roosevelt said, "Comparison is the thief of joy."
4. **Avoidance tactic.** Rather than proactively engaging with our challenging emotions or the struggles we might be experiencing, social media can serve as an avoidance strategy. When I am experiencing heightened feelings of anxiety, social media can almost numb those feelings. Clearly, this is an unhealthy way to manage feelings.
5. **Toxic debates.** Social media can encourage our worst traits and this can be seen most profoundly in those epic, circular debates about education.

Conversations about the more controversial aspects of education can become combative, entrenching people in their own views and closing minds.

Minimalist social media

Control is important when it comes to having a healthy relationship with social media. Newport recommends what he calls a digital declutter:

> *"It asks that you begin by taking a 30-day break from optional digital technologies in your personal life. These include any apps, services, or web sites that aren't necessary for your work or play a vital role in your daily routine. For most people, these optional technologies include social media, online news and entertainment sites, games and streaming videos."*

This digital declutter leaves you with a real understanding of what you want to keep in your life – and what you don't. A little space to reflect reveals just how much of our time is absorbed by social media and the impact it can have on us emotionally. When you first embark on the digital declutter, you will no doubt feel the absence of social media keenly and struggle to resist its addictive call. With time, however, resistance becomes much easier. You might begin to wonder why you have been devoting so much time to social media. And when the 30 days are up, you might be able to take a more disciplined approach.

If the digital declutter isn't for you, there are other ways to prevent social media from taking over your life:

1. **Don't try to keep up**. Social media never stops: it is a wheel that turns relentlessly. When I first used it in 2016, I couldn't believe that activity, discussion and debates about education were taking place at all times. It seemed ludicrous. The truth is that it is impossible to keep up with the tsunami of content. This advice from the website Zen Habits is very helpful: "Twitter is like a river ... you can step into it at any point and feel the water, bathe in it, frolic if you like ... and then get out. And go back in at any time, at any point. But, you don't have to try to consume the entire river – it's impossible and frankly a waste of time."[31]
2. **Control the apps**. Notifications and alerts can loudly shatter your concentration and make it harder to achieve your goals. They can mean that social media is in charge of you, rather than the other way round. I would argue against having any notifications; instead, check your

---

31   https://zenhabits.net/a-minimalists-guide-to-using-twitter-simply-productively-and-funly

accounts as little or as often as feels comfortable for you. Apps like Moment or Stay Focused can help you to maintain balance in your use of online tools.

Here's another useful quote from the Zen Habits website:

"Don't be on Twitter all the time. Some people have it open all the time – and that's fine if it works for you. Personally, I've found that if Twitter is open (or if Twitterific, my desktop Twitter program, is open) all the time, I have a hard time focusing on other work. So like I said, I close it most of the time and open it a few times a day to see what's going on. Mainly when I want to take a break. I only open it for a few minutes at most."

Inferiority anxiety

Finally, how can we stop ourselves from drifting into the comparative mindset that leads to feelings of inadequacy? Social media is carefully designed to feed this mindset: we try hard to build up a "following" and we fixate on our "popularity" – on how many likes or retweets we have gained. We might build a carefully curated online presence, one that speaks of professional and private success. But the comparative mindset always kicks in, as we see others who seem to be achieving so much more.

Social media turbocharges the comparative mindset. It is almost guaranteed to make us feel deficient – your worth is defined through your follower count. But are we really any happier or more content when we finally hit our follower target? Or do we immediately set our sights on a new goal?

So, how can we use social media in a positive and proactive manner? How can we make sure it is something that contributes to our lives, rather than making us feel inadequate?

1. **Contribute**. As a bystander, it is easy to use social media as a way to observe what everyone else is doing. This can make us feel isolated and inadequate. But by sharing our own thinking, ideas and content, we move beyond this and become active participants. I try to take an approach of "quiet" engagement, tweeting every couple of days or sharing other people's work. This makes me feel as if I am engaging in something that is useful and can support others. When you are using social media only to promote yourself, your own ideas or your own work, there is a risk of it becoming a vehicle for narcissism.
2. **Cultivate your self-esteem offline.** Don't rely on your online presence to give purpose and value to your life – it is never going to provide

that. Instead, allow space for the really important relationships: family, friends and colleagues. Use the self-compassion exercises from Part II of this book to create lasting feelings of self-worth and positivity. These feelings are so much more valuable that the fleeting hit you get when someone follows you back.

3. **Use social media mindfully**. One of the appealing elements of social media is the sense of getting lost in it and the fact that it appears to help us switch off. There is a full, empty feeling, however, that comes with too much scrolling. Being conscious of this, and frequently asking ourselves *why* we are using social media, is necessary to develop a healthy relationship with it.

Technology has the potential to enrich our lives and improve our classroom teaching. What this chapter has revealed, however, is that we need to be conscious and deliberate in the way we use it. Otherwise, we risk never being able to switch off from our teaching persona, which can increase feelings of stress and anxiety. A balanced approach to technology allows us to reap the rewards and maintain the positive outlook that we need in order to build our resilience.

Serene summary

The first step in having a healthy relationship with technology is to take control. Decide the approach you want to take to your work emails and be disciplined in sticking to it. Then, streamline your social media use. Only use it in a way that generates benefits for you and your wellbeing. Don't be lured into a comparative mindset – recognise that what you see is not an authentic version of someone's life or, indeed, their classroom.

13. TAKING A RESULTS PERSPECTIVE

Anxious anecdote

Jenny took a deep breath as she walked towards the hall, trying desperately to subdue the feelings of panic that knotted her stomach. Huddled inside the hall were groups of teenagers; nervous, excited chatter filled the air. Exam results day had arrived.

Jenny's anxiety had been building for days – time had seemed to slow to a crawl as results day approached. She had barely slept a wink the night before, owing to nightmares about hysterically crying teenagers and fellow teachers avoiding her gaze. At one point, the booming voice of her headteacher, his face purple with rage, had shaken her awake: "You will never teach an exam class in this school again!"

Inside the hall, she sought out the faces of her students, hoping to read their expressions. It was her first results day and one she was not likely to forget...

Every profession involves the expectation of results: there might be targets to work towards or some kind of performance evaluation. But for those of us who work in education, the word "results" is particularly significant, because it speaks of the results of the young people we teach.

These results can have a transformative impact on their futures, so the weight of this particular responsibility can be hard for teachers to bear. The reality is that the pressure of delivering exam results can lead to intense stress and anxiety. The huge volume of work that falls on teachers in the run-up to assessments and exams is then followed by a void, as our control vanishes and the onus falls completely on our students.

Performativity culture

Performativity is a term used by the education academic Stephen J Ball[32] to describe society's fixation with statistics, testing, grades and goals. In the context

---

32   www.tandfonline.com/doi/abs/10.1080/0268093022000043065

of education, "performativity" refers to a relentless focus on exam performance – one that leads to a culture of high scrutiny and teaching to the test.

Unfortunately, schools do exist in which every conversation comes back to exam results and the progress of students. They can be hugely dispiriting and soulless places to work in – the joy of education is lost in a spreadsheet drive for attainment. Such schools can also have an atmosphere of fear: anxiety is rife and creativity is not. In England, the correlation between exam performance and pay progression generates even more anxiety and stress for teachers.

The impact of performativity culture on our relationships with students can be profound. Rather than encouraging nurturing relationships that motivate young people to be the best versions of themselves, excessive accountability regimes lead to teachers projecting their stress on to students. Those feelings of anxiety may be exacerbated by leaders who project their own fears about the consequences of bad results on to everyone else in school. In 2018, Valentine Mulholland, who at the time was head of policy for the National Association of Head Teachers, told *The Guardian*:[33]

> *"In no other profession would you have that. You can have one year of pupils which is very different from previous years, which [headteachers] have no control over. If you live with that sword of Damocles over your head, it's difficult not to cascade that fear to the rest of your school."*

So, how can we prevent the pressure of accountability from overwhelming us?

Acceptance

Results will always be part of teaching, at all levels. The reality is that every generation has believed themselves to be at the mercy of an exam-obsessed culture, as this statement from 1960 reveals: "We live in a test-conscious, test-giving culture in which the lives of people are in part determined by their test performance."[34]

Rather than allowing results to ruin our experience of education, we need to accept the part they play in dictating our experiences in school. We have to be accountable – and so do students. Realising that results will never go away can help us to view them as the necessity that they are. And there are positives to results, the most obvious being the fact that they can enable a positive future for young people. It is wonderful when we see a student rewarded for all their hard work with the grade they have hoped for.

---

33   www.theguardian.com/education/2018/may/13/teacher-burnout-shortages-recruitment-problems-budget-cuts
34   Sarason et al, 1960, p26

Perspective

At first, as a new teacher, exam results feel like a reflection of our capacity to teach. As the years go by, they still matter and they still have the potential to cause sleepless nights, but they do not "belong" to us in the same way as those first results. Teachers do, of course, influence how well students do in exams and assessments – it would be utterly naive to claim that we don't. Yet, with time comes the understanding that we are just a small part of the big picture that determines a students' exam results.

The young people themselves are, of course, a much greater part of that picture, and those exam results are the product of an education that began when they were five years old. Remembering that – and focusing only on what we actually have control over – helps to make the pressure more manageable.

What we can control

A degree of peace comes from knowing we have done everything within our power to aid our students. That doesn't mean working 24 hours a day, seven days a week. Instead, it means taking a careful and practical look at how we can best use our time to support them.

The essential factors that pave the way for exam success are:

1. **Positive relationships**. Our students need to feel that we care about them and know them as individuals. If we show that we believe in them and are here to support them, they will be more motivated in our subject. It is important to remember that when we are relaxed, we are more approachable. It is also important to remember the power of humour to lift students out of their own feelings of anxiety. Positive relationships can facilitate another essential part of supporting students' exam success: open and transparent conversations. Appropriate pressure needs to be placed on young people, particularly in the case of apathetic teenagers. Questions need to be asked about lack of effort or missed homework tasks. These conversations are much easier if they take place in the context of a positive relationship based on respect and a desire for that young person to do well.

2. **Planning**. Instead of throwing everything we've got at end-of-year revision lessons, we need to think very carefully at the start of the school year about how we will use our time. That includes breaking down what students need to know and the time we have to teach it. Ideally, this is a collaborative process that involves the sharing of expertise throughout departments (in secondary schools) and among other teachers (in primaries). This approach allows us to take professional control over

exam pressures, so we are no longer at the mercy of another round of performance management. In many schools now, post-exam results analysis involves individual meetings, so the more information you have about what you've done to facilitate class and individual success, the less stressful these meetings will be. Evidence of a long-term action plan will be very helpful. This also has a beneficial impact on our resilience: the more detailed and practical the action plan is, the more likely we are to feel calm about the year ahead. Sharing this with students will also help them to facilitate their own success.

3. **Feedback**. Young people need feedback in order to improve, but delivering this can be very time-consuming. In chapter 21, we will look at strategies to limit the pressure that feedback places on us as teachers. Whatever strategies we employ, we need to make sure that students are clear on their current ability and what they need to do to get better. This gives them confidence and clarity, and helps to prepare them for exam or assessment situations.

4. **Collaboration and discussion**. It is so important that we seek help and support with exam or assessment classes. That comes in many different forms: informal conversations with colleagues about the best teaching approaches; support from heads of department regarding lack of effort or challenges; pastoral support with issues at home and a range of other factors. A lot can be gained from observing and learning from more experienced colleagues who consistently deliver good exam results with a range of cohorts. Ask to pop into a lesson and watch how they are teaching; ask them what their secrets are and be open to experimenting. Making the most of these support networks can keep us from becoming isolated in our own narratives of stress and pressure. It is also necessary to feed back to parents about a young person's progress. Often, we feel inclined towards optimism when talking to parents, but it is vital that we give an honest account of how their child is performing.

Results day

Chris Curtis, whom we met in chapter 8, has written a wonderful blog post about his approach to results day.[35] Here is an extract:

> *"Results day is about the students. It should only be about the students.*
> *A big clue about this fact is that we have results day when teachers are*

---

[35]   https://learningfrommymistakesenglish.blogspot.com/2016/08/public-displays-of-affection-floating.html

on holiday. What bigger message do you need that we need to place the students at the heart of things? Students mirror and copy our emotions. If our reaction to the results is over-the-top, then what is stopping them from copying our emotions, seeing the whole thing as success or failure, life or death or the beginning or the end? On a difficult day we want students to have clarity, perspective and thought and they will get that from the teachers and staff around them."

This highlights that we have a responsibility to model serenity and perspective, even if we might not be feeling it. It is natural to be nervous for our students, but bear in mind Chris's message: "Results day is about the students."

Learn from the results

Regardless of where we are in our teaching careers, we are still learning, growing and improving as time goes by. Exam results can be instrumental in facilitating that improvement and teachers should reflect carefully on the story they tell. Here are some ways to do this:

1. **How close to predictions?** Most schools ask for predictions of student performance. This helps us to recognise how well we know our students and our specifications. Obviously, the accuracy of our predictions will improve with experience, but we need to continually reflect on this. If we are way off, then we are not familiar enough with the content of our students' work or the specifications of the exam. Both need really careful scrutiny throughout the teaching year.
2. **Assess underperformance**. This needs to be done objectively, first with careful consideration of each student's experience. Some of the factors that might determine underperformance will be beyond our control, such as poor effort or issues at home. Then it is time to ask ourselves honest questions: could we have done anything differently to support the progress of that student? The same applies to groups of students: are any underperforming? If so, this may come back to aspects of classroom delivery and you may need to reflect further on differentiation. We will explore differentiation in detail in chapter 20.
3. **Examine national trends and exam reports**. We all want to be as empowered and as clear as possible on how we can improve our classroom provision. Lots of information is released after the exam period and it needs to be read and reflected upon. This is time well spent and it can alleviate some of those feelings of anxiety: you can take a deep breath and begin the whole process again much better informed.

Results matter – it is naive to suggest they don't. But, for the sake of our own sanity, we need to develop a healthy relationship with them. This will allow us be supportive and useful to the young people we teach.

Serene summary

First, we need to accept that results are always going to be a part of teaching. Focusing on the things we can influence – relationships, planning, collaboration and feedback – will allow us to feel that we have done all we can to facilitate students' success. Careful reflection will help us to improve our provision and the support we offer.

14. EXERCISE

Anxious anecdote

Breathing deeply, Bruce took a moment to appreciate the calm he felt flooding through his body. Thirty minutes earlier, he had been angrily changing into his running shorts, reflecting on the parental email that had ruined his day at school.

Giving precious Bartholomew a detention had apparently caused "significant upset" for this disruptive student. Bruce had been internally composing his reply for the rest of the day, detailing the significant upset Bartholomew had caused him by sticking a Post-it on his back that read "I smell".

But 30 minutes of what he liked to call "jog-walking" had allowed him to reach some kind of equilibrium – and to form a plan for what to do next.

Most people, when asked what might lessen their anxiety, are able to talk about the fact that exercise releases endorphins and makes us feel much better. We all know that exercise is important, but it can be challenging to find the motivation – and the time.

Throughout history, exercise has been recommended as a way of improving physical and mental health. Sushruta (also spelled Suśruta), an Indian physician in the sixth century BC, is credited with giving the first written prescription for exercise. Since then, exercise has become a staple remedy for feelings of anxiety and depression.

But fear not: this chapter will not be another diatribe about how you should immediately stop what you're doing and start training for a marathon. Nor will I instruct you to spend many hours a day engaging in a physical activity that you loathe. Both would have a negative impact, making you feel more frustrated and anxious as you struggled to build up an unsustainable habit.

Exercise needs to work for the individual: there is no universal prescription for the type or the amount. But before we explore the practicalities, it is worth detailing some of the reasons why exercise can help us to manage feelings of stress and anxiety.

1. **Positivity**. As in any profession, there are times when teachers have to dig deep to find motivation: first thing on a rainy morning, for example, when faced with a room full of apathetic teenagers who are unwilling to summon the brain power needed to tackle a poem. These young people need positivity, drive and enthusiasm to inspire them, but that can sometimes be hard for us to find. The positive endorphins released by exercise can be a quick fix – this is one reason why exercising in the morning can be hugely beneficial. I know I feel far more sluggish on the mornings when I haven't run to school (not as athletic as it sounds – school is only a few miles from my home!). Exercise is also an effective diversion from our own inner monologues, allowing us to focus instead on our physical feelings, our surroundings or the people we are exercising with.

2. **Sleep and relaxation**. Regular exercise helps us to sleep better and switch off from the teacher ruminations that keep us from relaxing. It has a magical ability to slow down our minds, allowing us to think with greater clarity and concentration. Apparently, exercise can also have a positive impact on our brain chemistry, increasing the availability of important anti-anxiety neurochemicals. I asked Zoe Enser, a former English teacher and school leader who is now a specialist English adviser for Kent, how she uses running to combat feelings of anxiety in her career: "I do exercise a lot, focusing on running distance, marathon and ultra-marathons, but also heading out every day when I can. I sometimes need to push myself harder than that, too, in order to 'clear' the feelings of anxiety from my system. A really tough class, or a session on the spin bike which gets my pulse rate up and sweat pouring, often makes me feel better. If I am concentrating on trying to get through the workout then I can't be overthinking other things."

3. **Self-esteem**. Anxiety and stress can chip away at our self-worth and make us question our competency. This leads us to work longer and longer hours, which makes us feel even more overwhelmed – and so the vicious circle continues. But exercise can help us to develop a more positive self-image and, in turn, build up our resilience. The teacher Steven Craig told me how exercise has been hugely beneficial for his own self-esteem: "CrossFit is great on a number of fronts. Exercising as part of a group has helped me to remember that a world beyond the classroom actually exists, and the social contact helps me to stay grounded while I face mountains of planning and marking. In addition, the opportunity to learn new skills and improve my fitness gives me a sense that I am growing in some way, becoming a better and more resilient person."

Find the exercise for you

Some people find it genuinely bizarre when I say that running is something I enjoy and carve out time for six days a week. My pupils are aghast when I tell them I usually run to and from work. Starting a running club at my school has helped some of them to see the benefits, but most still think it an odd habit!

Differentiation certainly applies to exercise, and the key is to find the right type of exercise for you. Simply walking for 30 minutes is an excellent form of exercise that can also clear the mind. The following quote is from *A Philosophy of Walking* by Frédéric Gros, a wonderful book on the pleasure of walking:

> *"Walking is the best way to go more slowly ... To walk, you need to start with two legs. The rest is optional. If you want to go faster, then don't walk, do something else: drive, slide or fly. Don't walk. And when you are walking, there is only one sort of performance that counts: the brilliance of the sky, the splendour of the landscape. Walking is not a sport."*

It might be that a competitive team sport is the best option for you. Or perhaps you might enjoy an individual sport like running or cycling. Or you might find that yoga or t'ai chi are the forms of exercise you prefer. Try out lots of different options to find the one that best fits your disposition and your schedule.

Tackling procrastination

"You could be good today, but instead you choose tomorrow," wrote Marcus Aurelius. The hardest part of establishing an exercise habit is taking the initial steps, as the urge to procrastinate strikes and we decide to put it off. We find excuses for why we cannot possibly exercise on this particular day.

For years, I worked in running shops. When customers asked me how to take a more structured approach to exercise, my advice was always the same: set a time of the day when you are going to exercise and stick to it. Even if the wind is howling and you feel exhausted, just go – don't overthink it. You may dread the prospect of it, but afterwards you will always feel better.

Then it is about *remembering* how you feel afterwards – the feeling that helps worries to drift away and makes you feel more positive about life. Exercising with others – by starting a teacher fitness club, for example – can help to make the habit sustainable, as others are relying on you to take part.

For those who want to build a running habit, some really great apps are available, such as Couch to 5K. You don't need any previous experience of running or any specialist clothes or equipment – you will progress slowly but surely, and after nine weeks you will be running 5K without stopping.

Setting a goal will help you to persevere when the going gets tough. For running, you might sign up to a 5K Parkrun.[36] Continue your exercise drive for at least a month: this will allow you to establish a structure and build a habit that is more likely to stick. The key is to get out there, no matter the weather!

Serene summary

There is no denying that exercise can be hugely beneficial when it comes to managing teacher anxiety and building resilience. The key is to find the right type of exercise for you. Then, to build a positive habit, you must be disciplined about setting a time and a routine for your exercise. Always bear in mind the positives – this will help you to sustain the habit when the going gets tough.

---

36   www.parkrun.org.uk

15. KEEP ON LEARNING

Anxious anecdote

Izzy was 10 years into her teaching career. Her teaching was fine, her classes behaved and her results were generally good. She was, however, beginning to feel restless and as if she needed a change. It had been a long time since she had tried anything different in her classroom.

She had always enjoyed writing, so one weekend Izzy decided to set up her own blog. She was pleased with the name she came up with: www.tenyearsateacher.co.uk. The aim was to reflect on what she had learned in those first 10 years and explore how she might overcome this latent boredom.

Izzy wanted to recapture the sense of boundless possibility that teaching had once offered her. Alongside the blog, she also set herself the target of reading at least one teaching book a month. Would this improve her teaching and how she felt about the profession?

Teachers are passionate about what they do. But sometimes, over time, that passion can subside and be replaced with lingering dissatisfaction. Anxiety and stress, as we have explored, can fuel those feelings: it is difficult to feel enthusiastic about our teaching if we are struggling to cope.

One way to stop focusing on those anxieties and find motivation is to build a meaningful reflection habit. Doing so can reveal patterns in our behaviour and working habits that may contribute to our feelings of anxiety. It also allows us to be perpetual students of our craft – we see teaching as something we can keep getting better at. As Daniel Goleman writes in *Emotional Intelligence*, this growth mindset is vital to building resilience:

> *"People's beliefs about their abilities have a profound effect on those abilities. Ability is not a fixed property; there is a huge variability in how you perform. People who have a sense of self-efficacy bounce back from failures; they approach things in terms of how to handle them rather than worrying about what can go wrong."*

125

Reading, learning and reflecting all boost our self-esteem. In 2016, I challenged myself to read 52 books over the year, to help me step out of myself and continue growing as a person and a professional. Meaningful individual reflection allows us to take ownership of our development and move forward positively.

Meaningful reflection can also stop us looking for quick fixes to apply in the classroom. As Dylan Wiliam said at a conference in 2010,[37] "Teachers are like magpies. They love picking up shiny little ideas from one classroom, taking it back to their classroom, trying it once, and then moving on to the next shiny idea."

Reflect, reflect, reflect

A key part of fostering resilience is the belief that we are developing as professionals. When we perceive ourselves as learners and recognise that we will always make mistakes, we are likely to be more secure in our teacher identities and therefore more resilient. Consider this quote from the basketball great Michael Jordan:

> "I've missed more than 9,000 shots in my career. I've lost almost 300 games. Twenty-six times I've been trusted to take the game winning shot and missed. I've failed over and over and over again in my life. And that is why I succeed."

Teaching is a remarkably complex, multifaceted skill and we never truly "master" it. Rather than being intimidating, this is actually one of the most energising things about the profession: we are always novices and this means teaching can be endlessly exciting. Remember also that teaching doesn't have to be formulaic – there are many different ways in which we can improve our provision for young people.

Realising this can reduce the stress and alleviate the competitive element of the job. The goal becomes more simple: to be one step better than you were before. What aspect of your teaching do you want to improve on?

Writing for reflection

Writing is an ideal tool for reflection: it is an easy and effective way to offload some of our internal baggage. As Anne Frank wrote, "Paper has more patience than people." Regularly recording your thoughts can help you to track your progress and make informed decisions about how to move forward. Writing a diary is one option, or you might prefer to join the huge number of teachers sharing their ideas more publicly in online blogs (anonymous or otherwise).

---

37   https://youtu.be/wKLo15A80lI

If you are dealing with stress, for example, recording your thoughts over time could allow you to identify the source of the stress and what you might do to cope. Or, if you are considering your students' understanding of your subject, you might reflect on your ability to give clear explanations, and then experiment with pace and the words you use.

In his autobiography, *On the Move*, Oliver Sacks writes about his journalling habit:

> *"I started keeping journals when I was fourteen and at last count had nearly a thousand. They come in all shapes and sizes, from little pocket ones which I carry around with me to enormous tomes. I always keep a notebook by my bedside, for dreams as well as night time thoughts, and I try to have one by the swimming pool or the lakeside or the seashore; swimming too is very productive of thoughts which I must write, especially if they present themselves, as they sometimes do, in the form of whole sentences or paragraphs.*
>
> *"But for the most part, I rarely look at the journals I have kept for the greater part of a lifetime. The act of writing is itself enough; it serves to clarify my thoughts and feelings. The act of writing is an integral part of my mental life; ideas emerge, are shaped, in the act of writing. My journals are not written for others, nor do I usually look at them myself, but they are a special, indispensable form of talking to myself."*

As well as providing clarity, writing can also help us to notice and appreciate the positives that might be less immediately apparent. In an article for the journal *Reflective Practice*, the educator Claire Goodley argues that reflective writing can help teachers to develop the art of "noticing":

> *"The discipline of noticing their own practice from a professional and personal perspective can allow a teacher to turn negative feelings into positive disruptions. Teachers may be measured and judged, but the process of noticing can be more effective to their sense of professionalism than action research, as they are capable of changing themselves, and their practice. It is possible to make the experience of being a teacher more positive, through noticing tensions and drilling down into the core reason for them, rather than finding a convenient label and dismissing it as a part of the role that is out of their control."*

Dr Lucy Kelly has researched the impact of reflective writing on teacher wellbeing. She sent me a summary of the findings of the research:

Reimagining the Diary project

Led by Dr Lucy Kelly (School of Education, University of Bristol) with Dr Catherine Kelly (School of Law, University of Bristol) and Stand + Stare (creative partners).

The Reimagining the Diary project (currently funded by Brigstow and ESRC IAA) explores reflective practice (e.g. reflective diary writing/journalling) as a positive tool for individual teacher wellbeing. In a profession recognised as one of the most "stressful",[38] this practice might be a "small, but important, step"[39] in addressing the current wellbeing crisis within the sector.

In both phases,[40] we worked with a group of 15 teachers at various stages of their career, and with differing levels of experience. In Phase 1, participants chose a diary – plain notebook, kindness jotter, sound journal – and kept it for a week during term time, before reflecting on the process via an online survey. Participants' entries were not analysed because we wanted the reflections to be as authentic as possible.

Notwithstanding the limitations of our study – including sample size and duration – our results reveal that over 93% of participants perceived an improvement in their wellbeing when keeping a diary, using it as a tool for celebration and catharsis and an opportunity to look at an event or situation from different perspectives. Despite time being the biggest factor to consider, 86.7% of the group would advise other teachers to keep a diary, and 60% said that they would continue this practice.[41]

In terms of catharsis, the diary was "a safe place to explore your world"[42] because it helped participants turn the abstract into the "concrete",[43] making it much easier to deal with. Extracting thoughts and feelings on to the page encouraged users to separate themselves from the day's experiences; writing became "a release … somewhere for your thoughts to go, because they don't

38   Holmes, E (2019). *A Practical Guide to Teacher Wellbeing*, SAGE Publications, p.20
39   Kelly, L. (2020) "Reclaiming teacher wellbeing through reflective diary writing", *Impact* 9, https://impact.chartered.college/article/reclaiming-teacher-wellbeing-reflective-diary-writing
40   What follows is taken from: Kelly, L. (2020) "Reclaiming teacher wellbeing through reflective diary writing", *Impact* 9; and Kelly, L. (Due 2021) "Writing wellbeing: using reflective diary-writing to support English teacher wellbeing", in Watson, A and Newman, R (eds), *A Practical Guide to Teaching English in the Secondary School*, second edition, Routledge
41   Kelly, L. (2020) "Reclaiming teacher wellbeing through reflective diary writing", *Impact* 9, https://impact.chartered.college/article/reclaiming-teacher-wellbeing-reflective-diary-writing
42   Johnstone, C. (2018) *Dare to be Happier: an introduction to the power of journaling*, Snowdrop Press, p.xvii
43   Hayes, MC. (2018) *Write Yourself Happy: the art of positive journalling*, Octopus Publishing Group, p.46

normally go anywhere else".[44] Furthermore, the diary had a therapeutic quality, acting as a "venting tool".[45] Interestingly, although time was the biggest factor, participants felt "bereft" if a day was missed, recognising the extra "thoughts charging around" that hadn't been "processed".[46]

Using the diary as "a stress buster"[47] to reflect on the working day (which 86.7% did) helped participants position themselves at the centre of their own "narratives",[48] because "teachers ... need an outlet as we are also people with lives and worries".[49] Indeed, the diary was an opportunity "to switch off"[50] and insert boundaries in a profession without any.[51]

Yet our findings also reveal that teachers must document positive emotions and experiences too – such as "moments ... enjoyed in the classroom".[52] This celebratory practice improves self-esteem and self-confidence[53] because it refocuses teachers' attention on to what *is* going well in the classroom and beyond – however small – instead of what isn't.

This links to perspective – the final key theme from Phase 1. The diary enabled participants to reconnect to their "why"[54] and what teaching meant to them, personally, including their aspirations and "philosophy".[55]

Yet, our Phase 1 survey data demonstrated that reflective practice, like wellbeing, is bespoke. To move the project forward, we had to consider a format that wasn't prescribed but still offered structure and choice to those who needed it. Furthermore, if we were asking teachers to devote some of their limited time to reflection, then the format had to be aesthetically pleasing, accessible, non-judgemental and non-expectant. The idea of it being a private, slow space was also important: how could we help teachers slow down and bookend their day in an engaging, meaningful way?

44 Reimagining the Diary focus group, University of Bristol, May 2019. Data available on formal request
45 Ibid.
46 Reimagining the Diary survey, University of Bristol. Data available on formal request
47 Ibid.
48 Carr, D. (2006) "Moral education at the movies: on the cinematic treatment of morally significant story and narrative", *Journal of Moral Education* 35:3, p320
49 Reimagining the Diary survey, University of Bristol. Data available on formal request
50 Ibid.
51 Kelly, L. (Due 2021) "Writing wellbeing: using reflective diary-writing to support English teacher wellbeing", in Watson, A and Newman, R (eds), *A Practical Guide to Teaching English in the Secondary School*, second edition, Routledge
52 Reimagining the Diary survey, University of Bristol. Data available on formal request
53 Hayes, MC. (2018) *Write Yourself Happy: the art of positive journalling*, Octopus Publishing Group
54 Howard, K. (2020) *Stop Talking About Wellbeing: a pragmatic approach to teacher workload*, John Catt
55 Reimagining the Diary survey, University of Bristol. Data available on formal request

From these musings the research team came up with the Diary Toolkit: a smorgasbord of reflective practice. The Toolkit reimagines, and reclaims, the loaded term "diary"[56] for 21st-century teachers. The Toolkit moves beyond the traditional written diary format, reimagining it into a multi-modal, playful and creative space where participants are encouraged to try out a range of reflective activities, including: storyboarding, audio recording, free writing, doodling and affirmation writing. The Toolkit also includes "transition" and "reflection" phases. Before completing the main activity, participants use a spinner/dice to decide on a mindfulness practice – such as drinking a hot beverage slowly or listening to a favourite piece of music – to encourage a reflective mode of thinking. The "reflection" stage invites participants to reflect on what they would like to do with the main activity – share, archive, use or destroy – in order to question the audience and purpose of the diary and, perhaps, to let go of prior expectations.

Participants kept the Toolkit for a week during the spring term and were asked to try – and reflect on – each main activity once. The "transition" and "reflection" stages were also included. As with Phase 1, personal entries weren't looked at, but a detailed survey was completed to gather views. Initial feedback on the Diary Toolkit is very positive: 93% of participants preferred it to another diary format and 86% would like to continue using it. Most teachers enjoyed the range of reflective practices: it was playful and creative, while providing structure for those participants who, having had a full day in school, didn't want to make further decisions.

Additionally, 71% of participants would recommend the Toolkit to other teachers and, although time was still the main factor (alongside Covid-19 and lockdown), 93% liked the "transition" stage because it helped them to separate school/home and ritualise reflective practice. Participants praised the positive impact the Toolkit had on their wellbeing, too. As one individual summarised: "I came into this project last year imagining that a diary entry was just about writing about what happened that day. My eyes have now been opened to a plethora of reflective activities that have helped me keep sane!"[57]

In Phase 3, we are working with new teachers for longer periods of time. Participants will create their own custom-made Diary Toolkit

---

56   Kelly, L, Huxford, G and Kelly, C. (2020) "'In our daily struggles': diaries as a tool for teacher well-being", *Life Writing*, pp.1-16 (published online)

57   Reimagining the Diary survey, University of Bristol, April 2020. Data available on formal request

(physical and/or digital) based on their favourite activities. We really hope this bespoke approach to reflective practice will help teachers reclaim the diary as a space for their personal and professional selves to flourish.

Reading for reflection

Today, a vast range of educational books are available, as well as a growing body of research that can encourage a more thoughtful approach to teaching. Reading widely can help you to consider your own teaching more critically and engage with the many levels of learning.

In his book *Norwegian Wood,* the Japanese writer Haruki Murakami highlights that reading should be diverse: "If you only read the books that everyone else is reading, you can only think what everyone else is thinking." There can be a tribe mentality among teachers, but we should always try to broaden our pedagogical horizons, not limit them.

Reading one book a term can provide a roadmap – as you read, you can experiment in your classroom and consider the impact. It can be very motivating to witness the small gains in your teaching as you continue to build your repertoire of skills.

Coaching for reflection

Coaching can be a powerful way to help you develop professionally. Andy Buck, a former headteacher and author of a range of education books, sent me his reflections on how his BASIC coaching model (explored in his excellent book *The BASIC Coaching Method*), can help to build teacher resilience:

"One of the greatest benefits from adopting a coaching approach to conversations is how it leaves others thinking and feeling about the future. When individuals have had the opportunity to reflect on their current situation, decide what they want to achieve and have an ownership of what can be done to move forward, they are inevitably more committed to the way ahead. It is a powerful way to build personal resilience and ability to bounce back during difficult times.

This approach has two key advantages:

1. It leaves individuals feeling clearer about the future. From clarity comes resilience.
2. It increases a sense of personal optimism about the future and about what is possible.

One of the biggest risks in us just giving other people advice, rather than letting them come up with solutions for themselves, is that we devise ideas which would work for us as individuals and for the situation we find ourselves in, rather than solutions for someone else and the situation they are in. It also runs the risk of leaving people feeling disempowered and rather helpless. Neither are helpful when trying to build personal resilience.

This idea applies to the world of work as well as to everyday life. When you are having conversations with colleagues, the more you are able to help them reflect and come up with their own ideas, the greater ownership they will have. Of course, it can be very tempting for us to suggest the answer, especially when we really want to help.

There are four key elements to the BASIC coaching method:

1. **BASIC Steps**: a suggested structure to conversations.
2. **BASIC Qualities**: what are you like to talk to?
3. **BASIC Habits**: remembering these can make your conversations even more productive.
4. **BASIC Feedback**: a powerful way to have conversations about performance.

The BASIC Steps are the five broad stages within a conversation (see below). It is important to say right from the outset that these five steps really must be seen as a broad framework rather than a narrow set of steps that must always be followed in exactly the same order."

If your school doesn't have a formal coaching structure, you could look at establishing an informal coaching relationship with a colleague. Sometimes we need others to guide our thinking through questioning and probing, and a coaching relationship can motivate you to improve.

Regular reading and experimenting in the classroom has certainly energised my teaching. It has also shown me how vital it is that teachers are given space to reflect. The more we can make teaching an intellectually stimulating profession, the more we will motivate, inspire and retain teachers in the profession. More importantly, the more we will continue to hone and improve our practice, leading to better experiences and outcomes for young people.

Setting goals

A key quality of resilient individuals is their ability to set meaningful goals. These goals help to sustain focus on improvement in the classroom, but they need to be realistic.

My goal for the next academic year, for example, is to experiment with more aspects of minimalism in my classroom, in order to improve students' concentration and my work-life balance. These are tangible outcomes that I can track throughout the year. I will use my blog to reflect on progress and ask learners how they have found the process.

History is full of examples of people who have cultivated success through discipline, learning and effort. Abraham Lincoln, for example, was born in a log cabin in a remote part of Kentucky. He had just one year of schooling, which he described as "defective". Lincoln embarked instead on a journey of self-improvement and continuous growth, ultimately becoming the 16th president of the US. Channelling some of Lincoln's spirit can keep us motivated, passionate and driven to do our best for young people.

Serene summary

Reflection and continual improvement is what keeps us passionate about teaching. Finding the reflection tool that works best for you – reading, writing or coaching – will ensure that you commit to it over time.

16. COLLABORATION

Anxious anecdote

"If you need anything at all, just ask."

Jerome played the words of his previous head of department in his mind. This hadn't been an empty platitude: it was a genuine philosophy of how she approached teaching and ran her department. No question was ever too simplistic; no request for support or help was ever denied. She did everything she could to pull the team together.

Six months earlier, Jerome had moved to a new school for his first position with responsibility. In just six months, this collaborative spirit in his previous school – which was one of the main reasons why he had found so much success in his first three years of teaching – had become nothing but a distant memory.

His new department, with 10 members of staff, was fiercely individualistic. Nobody discussed how they approached teaching; nobody discussed how to spark young people's enthusiasm in science. Doors to classrooms remained firmly closed.

Jerome felt his anxiety, which had always lingered, beginning to grow. He felt cut adrift and was starting to doubt himself. More pressing, however, was a deep sense of loneliness.

Anyone who has experienced any kind of mental health issue knows how hugely isolating it can feel. Some of us are lucky enough to have people around us who understand and encourage us to take the necessary steps to help ourselves. They nudge, cajole and guide us into moving forward. Without this, we can spiral into deeper feelings of anxiety and depression.

In the school context, we need similar emotional support. The difficulties and challenges we face, the anxieties we feel, can become so much more pervasive if we are in an isolating and unsupportive environment.

Teaching is interesting in this regard: we are surrounded by huge numbers of people and by endless communication, but it can be a lonely profession. Our physical distance from colleagues means that often we go for hours without any adult interaction. Our continual communication with young people involves a different power dynamic and requires a professional mask.

Given this, collaboration is profoundly important for wellbeing and resilience at every stage of a teacher's career. It is integral to building trust and positive relationships at all levels of the school community. As Daniel Goleman notes in *Emotional Intelligence*, "We are all wired to connect." That means we must seek out opportunities to share and connect with colleagues.

New teachers often require reassurance and a supportive community as they traverse unfamiliar and complex ground. Connection and collaboration are vital means of emotional aid in the early years of teaching.

More experienced teachers often require sustenance – they need to feel part of a team drive to help young people to achieve. No matter how long we have been teaching, we all need support from those around us and we all benefit from collaboration that can refine our teaching practice, as well as our work-life balance.

Making connections

In Johann Hari's book about anxiety and depression, *Lost Connections*, his central argument is very simple: the current epidemic of depression and anxiety exists, to a significant degree, because we have lost the art of connection: "We – without ever quite intending to – have become the first humans to dismantle our tribes. As a result, we have been left alone on a savanna we do not understand, puzzled by our own sadness."

This connection is even more important for teachers at the start of their careers, particularly in order to sustain positivity and resilience.

The culture of a school is hugely important. The answers to two important questions give a clear indication of how collegiate a school is. Are staff encouraged to seek each other out and discuss teaching and learning? And are mechanisms in place to encourage peer support and the sharing of best practice?

Building positive relationships, with colleagues and students, is key to maintaining resilience and optimism in our profession. The more those relationships involve trust, security and support, the more we are able to cope with the unpredictable challenges that an ordinary day in school can throw at us. Positive relationships within school and outside school can keep us from catastrophising and internalising our problems. Rather, they can help us to take ourselves less seriously in our earnest quest to be as good as we can be.

But some school cultures seem to actively discourage collaboration. There are schools where individual ownership of results is discussed more than any collegiate attempts to improve attainment (we will explore the traits of toxic environments in the next chapter).

Teachers are, of course, very busy, with many conflicting demands on their time. Our working lives are dictated by the school bell, making collaboration and opportunities to engage in prolonged discussions harder to come by. These time constraints and pressures can lead us to hunker down and simply try to get through the content.

A teacher who asked to remain anonymous told me about her experience of trying to manage her NQT year in an environment that lacked collaborative support:

"After qualifying I started my NQT year at a new school. I very quickly burned out. My teaching style didn't fit with what they wanted to see. I was tired all the time. I never felt like I was enough. Behaviour management felt impossible. There was increasing social tension within the department. My anxiety started to rise. I remember thinking, 'How can I keep it together in front of students? How can I be tough enough to discipline students while feeling hollow inside and ready to crumble?' There was also a range of wider school issues, lots of change for the whole school, and instability and uncertainty. I finished my NQT year and put it down as a bad year (other experienced teachers had felt the same)."

This account illustrates just how profoundly important it is that teachers work in a collegiate environment that considers the needs of others. This teacher's reflection on struggling to find the strength to deal with students in such an unsupportive environment is particularly revealing.

Why collaborate?

Andy Hargreaves is an education policy adviser and has written more than 30 books on education. The theme of collaboration in schools is central to his writing, in particular the following questions: why should we collaborate? How do people collaborate? What kinds of collaboration are more effective than others?

In a contribution to the book *Critical Discourses on Teacher Development*, Hargreaves listed 11 benefits of collaboration among school staff: moral support; increased efficiency; improved effectiveness; reduced overload; synchronised time perspectives between teachers and administrators; situated certainty of collective professional wisdom; political assertiveness; increased capacity for reflection; organisational responsiveness; opportunities to learn; and continuous learning.

In terms of student outcomes, research conducted around the world has also highlighted that collaboration can drive positive results. In a paper, the researchers Beatrice Avalos-Bevan and Martín Bascopé wrote: "Informal learning through teacher collaboration has been recognised as important in international research, for example, in the OECD directed TALIS study which found that collaboration connected with higher levels of teacher self-efficacy in almost all participating countries as well as with higher job satisfaction in two out of three countries."

Informal collaboration

Informal collaboration really matters in schools. This is the support that teachers offer each other that is not dictated by meetings, management or targets. As we learned in Part II of this book, seeking to encourage, motivate and communicate with those around us is vital not only for their wellbeing, but for our own.

All this can be facilitated by department heads, but the reality is that the best collaboration in schools is often spontaneous and driven by an innate human need for interaction. Informal collaboration can take several forms:

1. **Content conversations**. In the two years that I ran a podcast for *Tes* on English teaching, I felt hugely energised about how I was approaching my subject. Every month, I would spend an hour speaking to someone who was an expert on an aspect of English teaching; this would have a real impact on the ideas and content in my own lessons. Teachers love to discuss the different ways of approaching content and having those conversations will always be worthwhile. This can create open and resilient departments where every member of staff is a stakeholder in the goal of moving forward learning. That, after all, is our central purpose in the classroom. In staff meetings, there would be so much more energy if the discussion focused on teaching content, rather than managerial matters. Its absence from meetings, however, means we need to proactively seek out our colleagues and these conversations.
2. **Behaviour approaches**. We will explore this in greater detail in chapter 18, but a collaborative approach to behavioural issues is powerful and effective. This might involve sharing strategies with colleagues who also teach that particular child, or pulling together to support teachers who have challenging students. For various reasons, sometimes we need to remove a young person from a classroom – knowing that our colleagues will support us on this is hugely important.
3. **Checking in**. Of course, in the context of resilience and wellbeing, checking in with colleagues is vital. We must be sensitive to others in our departments or schools, asking after each other and listening to

each other. This can make such a positive difference to our experience of teaching. Some people are gifted at presenting a front, so we must be active in seeking to understand the reality of that person's experience. Schools should do all they can to nurture these networks, not remove them.

Formal collaboration

Although informal collaboration contributes significantly to school ethos and staff morale, formal collaboration also has huge potential to improve the staff experience and drive forward the provision for young people.

For formal collaboration to work, it is necessary to appreciate the fact that people are very different in their dispositions, and in how they like to work and think. A failure to recognise this can lead to resentment among staff and generate more anxiety, owing to arguments when people do not take ownership of what they are expected to. In my previous book, *A Quiet Education*, I wrote about this need for interpersonal sensitivity: we must be aware of how our colleagues work best and make space for quieter collaborative approaches.

Cross-department collaboration can work very well, with staff from different departments or parts of the school joining together to work on a particular project. In his book *The Thinking School*, the executive headteacher Dr Kulvarn Atwal explains that this is the principle for development in his schools:

> *"In the thinking school, all teachers are engaged with research; sometimes individually, but mostly collaboratively. They investigate their own and each other's practice in the quest for continual improvement. The learning environment encourages engagement in research, and provides resources for teachers to undertake it effectively."*

Another example of more formal collaboration is the Lesson Study approach,[58] a Japanese model of teacher-led research. This involves teachers working as a triad and specifying an area for development in their students' learning. The participants collaboratively plan, teach and observe a series of lessons. This enables them all to benefit from detailed discussion and receive feedback on this aspect of learning.

Ask for help

A core feature of resilient people in any workplace is that they are not afraid to ask for help. In a profession as varied and complex as teaching, we need to be proactive in seeking out advice and guidance from others.

---

58   https://tdtrust.org/what-is-lesson-study

Openness and transparency are also crucial to teacher wellbeing. Asking a colleague for assistance and going over the content with them, or requesting that they pop into a lesson to give feedback, can help us to overcome anxieties or concerns about the work we do in our classrooms. This can also help to inspire a more collaborative ethos and a positive sense of teacher identity.

Other networks

There are many ways in which teachers can network and collaborate outside of school. Twitter, of course, can enable us to connect with thousands of other teachers and can offer motivation and inspiration on many different levels. Reading and engaging with teacher blogs and podcasts offer similar benefits.

Building staff communities and an ethos of togetherness helps to make teaching a more manageable and enjoyable profession. Finding the collaboration method that works for you and your disposition is an important part of developing professional satisfaction.

Serene summary

Collaboration is vital for teacher wellbeing and can help to alleviate stress and anxiety. It requires teachers to be proactive and open, and to recognise that time spent speaking to a colleague will have more of a positive impact than time spent marking yet another piece of work. Schools should facilitate collaboration that involves the sharing of strategies and allows staff to focus on what matters: what happens in our classrooms.

17. LEAVING TOXIC ENVIRONMENTS

Anxious anecdote

8.15am. Zane's door opened without warning. Thomas, the school's deputy headteacher (a man who had been teaching for a grand total of five years), stood with a clipboard and one of the colour-coded spreadsheets that seemed to be an extension of his extremely expensive suit.

"Good morning, Mr Salidho. I'm here to talk to you about uploading lesson plans."

Zane's heart sank. Here it was: the weekly conversation about how his lesson plans lacked differentiation, detail and specific lesson objectives and, of course, how they weren't uploaded on time.

"In our weekly leadership team meeting your name was discussed again. Upon reviewing your lesson plans, it has been decided that they are lacking in differentiation, detail and specific lesson objectives. I am sure you are also aware that the lesson plans for the week need to be uploaded by 8am on a Monday morning.

"I have taken the liberty of printing off some exemplar lesson plans from the system for you to reflect further on. I think it would be prudent for us to meet after school today to discuss how best you might implement some of the good practice. Please be at my office at 4.30."

With that, Thomas spun around on his well-heeled shoes and vanished.

Picking up the huge pile of exemplar lesson plans, Zane saw that they were annotated to within an inch of their life, to explicitly outline what the lesson was doing effectively...

Toxic school environments very much exist in the UK. They are hidden from the public eye and from superficial inspection regimes, but the harsh reality is that things are happening in schools that destroy teaching careers. There are cultures of bullying, Orwellian degrees of scrutiny and obsessive fixations on external perceptions. Sometimes, as in any profession, it is the people least suited to leadership who make it to the top, and they rarely use their power to improve things for the people further down the hierarchy.

The impact of such toxic environments on individual teachers can be profound. Scores of enthusiastic and talented people are leaving the profession, burnt out and disillusioned.

I morphed into a version of Thomas, the well-heeled senior leader in this chapter's Anxious Anecdote, early in my teaching career. I joined a large leadership team at the end of my second year of teaching, earning a ludicrously high salary at an academy in central London. When the headteacher said in the interview, "I expect blood," I should have run a country mile. Instead, in youthful arrogance, I sacrificed my health and relationships and worked well over 80 hours a week: six days a week in school.

I look back and cringe: I fully assimilated myself into a toxic environment. As pressure was exerted on me, I tried to absorb it, but I know that I passed far too much pressure on to other members of staff, encouraging them to work unsustainably, too.

With my clipboard and an expensive black suit, I conducted conversations that left people in tears. I held intense weekly "workbook reviews"; I strolled in and out of lessons at whim; I expected more and more from the staff I managed. Everything they did was under scrutiny – we even held a weekly "premises check" on a Friday evening, to monitor and feed back on how presentable the classrooms were.

The truth was that the wellbeing of the people I managed was a lesser concern for me than the attainment of their students.

I spent two years feeling hugely uncomfortable and completely out of my depth. When I eventually had a breakdown, I knew that, in part, it was because I was being asked to act in a manner that was entirely against my disposition.

I handed in my notice in the January of my second year in the role and, despite six months of difficult experiences, I stayed until the end of the school year. I have no desire to recount those experiences here; suffice it to say that I am a different person as a result. They have left me with a real understanding of negative school environments and the impact they can have on mental health – from the point of view of the teacher and of the leader complicit in such toxicity.

It took me some time to channel those experiences into something positive. For a long time, I entirely lacked confidence and operated in a heightened state of anxiety and fear. The adage that difficulty builds our resilience is true, but the saying "What doesn't kill us makes us stronger" is too trite to throw around. It doesn't acknowledge that it can take a very long time for bad experiences to breed strength.

What constitutes a toxic environment?

No school is perfect and, of course, to some extent a person's experience of a school is subjective. Headteachers can exploit that subjectivity, making it harder to tackle toxic environments. When leaders are challenged, the response is usually along the lines of: what doesn't work for one teacher might allow another to thrive. This is why it is important to identify the common characteristics of toxic schools, to ensure that teachers and leaders can recognise when their school environment is unhealthy.

The terms "toxic school culture" and "toxic schools" are predominantly used to describe schools with aspects that negatively affect the performance, mental health or working environment of staff. The core issue is the direct and lasting impact that these negative experiences at work can have on our lives as a whole.

These negatives can be hard to spot: they often become norms that are deeply assimilated into the culture of the school. They can become invisible. But staff morale will reveal their existence: the staff will be constantly stressed and have little time to enjoy the benefits – professional and personal – of working with others. Staff turnover is another significant indicator of a toxic environment: low turnover speaks of commitment to and appreciation of the school ethos; high turnover reveals deep levels of dissatisfaction across the whole organisation.

One of the most significant characteristics of a toxic school is a culture of fear. There is a lack of trust between teachers and leaders. Staff feel vulnerable and constantly on edge; they feel as if they are under surveillance and don't have any space to do what they feel is right in the classroom. The voices of staff are not heard, or are heard only in a tokenistic way. The culture of fear is characterised by a lack of empathy and a lack of awareness of what staff might be experiencing.

Surviving in a toxic environment

In toxic schools, the more experienced staff members, who might be more inclined to voice their concerns, are often forced out, replaced by a small army of young teachers who are perceived by the school to be disposable and more compliant. Less experienced staff may not recognise that some of the practices that exist in the school are deeply dysfunctional. They will also be worried about passing their NQT year and of how it might look if they leave the school early. In teaching, a reference is vital and headteachers in toxic schools will seek to exploit this.

If you feel like you are working in a toxic school, it is so important that you are as open as you can be about your concerns. Find a member of staff whom you trust and share your thoughts – the chances are you will realise you are not alone in feeling that something is not right in your school. Make sure, however, that you take the time to build this relationship before revealing your feelings in depth.

Alongside this, try to find out about cultures in other schools: speak to the teachers you know in other environments and find out what their experience is like. This will help you to decide if it is the case that the school is the wrong fit for you.

There are numerous accounts online of working in toxic schools. The fact that they are often anonymous highlights just how difficult it is for teachers to talk honestly about their experiences. The example below, from an article on the Teachwire website,[59] encapsulates the mindset that begins to take over in a toxic environment: you work harder and harder and sacrifice everything else, in a blind attempt to keep up with unrealistic expectations.

> *"I stopped sleeping and my insomnia heightened my sense of insecurity. Being signed off work by the doctor forced me to re-evaluate my life and I promised my wife I would look for work at another school. When I told the headteacher, she told me she could make sure I never worked again."*

To prevent this mindset, it is so important to keep perspective. Remember that what is being asked of you is unrealistic and unsustainable. Be strong enough to put your own needs first – and that includes implementing any of the strategies that we have explored in this book. Set boundaries about how much work you are willing to do and stick to them. Even something as simple as not working through your lunch break is important, giving you space and allowing you to recharge your batteries.

There are also ways in which you can take ownership of boosting your own self-worth. You might share resources on Twitter, start a club for kids that involves an activity you love, or try to foster more community spirit within your department.

Write everything down

I cannot stress this point enough: in a toxic environment, it is crucial to make notes of everything that goes on. Every difficult conversation and every challenging meeting. Make sure that only you can access these notes – don't leave them lying around or on a school computer. Then, if you experience any issues regarding references or further employment, you will have a log of all that has happened in that context.

---

59   www.teachwire.net/news/the-school-i-taught-in-was-a-toxic-work-environment

If your situation does become very challenging, you must engage union support. The unions exist for a reason: to put the needs of staff first and provide them with external support. Some schools do all they can to quash union representation, but it is our legal right to take advice from them. Make sure you know who your union representative is and be proactive in seeking them out for discussions.

Moving schools

It is immensely dispiriting when teachers decide to leave the profession after working in only one school. Schools are their own little universes – there are profound differences between them and the ways in which they function. A bad experience at one school does not reflect the profession as a whole; rather, it is a sign that you do not fit in that particular culture. Be brave, be bold, and take your time to find an environment that works better for you.

I don't believe in regrets, but I do wish I hadn't rushed to take the first job I applied for on my training year. I was moving from Newcastle to London and my wife had already secured employment, so I needed a teaching job. I had never been in a London school and had no idea how they functioned. The huge recruitment process the school was going through, and the sheer number of teachers there on interview day, should have been a warning, but I was just thankful for the opportunity.

No school is perfect and to suggest so would be naive. It is so important, however, to scrutinise carefully all aspects of the school. Every school is trying to project an image of success and to lure parents and teachers. Reading through a school's website can be revealing to an extent: does it present a mission statement and purpose? What is the language like in relation to work-life balance? Consider what is missing: are there any staff testimonials? Is there a dedicated page concerning staff? And how many staff vacancies are there?

It is important to read inspection reports, but they need to be taken at face value. Plenty of schools that have a glossy "outstanding" banner hanging outside the building are deeply dysfunctional. What is the narrative around development? What comments are made about leaders?

The internet is, of course, full of ways to rate and review schools. Have a careful and considered look around, but always be mindful of the context of reviews. If it's a Mumsnet thread, for example, it will come from a completely different angle than a conversation on Twitter. And remember: much like restaurant reviews, people aren't necessarily going to go to the effort of leaving feedback if their experience was positive.

Try to find someone who works or has worked at the school you are applying to – they will be able to give you the inside track on the school environment. Their perspective will be authentic, but remember that it will also be entirely subjective.

The interview

An interview is as much about a school deciding if you fit with their values as it is about you deciding whether the school fits with yours. But, in the rush to secure a job, this is often overlooked: the pragmatic need for security overtakes niggling doubts that might exist on interview day. I know that was the case for me.

The first step in finding an environment that suits you is considering your core values. What kind of culture do you want to work in? And what kind of culture do you want to avoid? Here are some other ways to help you find the right fit:

1. **Be open-minded**. Think about the version of the school that is being presented to you. Are you being shown the reality of what it would be like to work there day in, day out? Have you been able to look around the school and see lessons taking place? If a tour has not been arranged, I would ask for one – you need to see what the school looks like in full flow. But remember that these tours can be carefully orchestrated to show you only the bright spots of a school environment.
2. **Ask questions**. Preparing a list of questions before the interview will ensure that you get all the information you need. There is a balance to be found here: only ask appropriate questions and only ask the appropriate people. It might make you nervous to ask questions, but any good leader will be happy to provide more information and address any concerns.
3. **Ask for time to think**. In the intensity of an interview day, we sometimes feel pressured into making a decision. This in itself is not a good sign: schools should be respectful of the fact that you might need time to consider an offer. It can take courage and conviction to say no, but if you have reflected carefully and your gut feeling is negative, then the chances are that it is not the school for you.

Recovering from a toxic school

Sometimes we need to hit rock bottom in order to re-evaluate and start again. Trauma as a result of work-based experiences is far more common in education than we might think. It can be difficult to accept that you might be suffering as a result of trauma: I know I tried to tell myself that my experience wasn't "that bad" and that others go through far worse. But, over time, I have come to accept that trauma as a result of school practices is a very real thing.

If this is something you have experienced, communication is key. It is essential that you remain open about how you are feeling with colleagues, friends and family. To recover from your experience, sometimes it is not as simple as merely moving to another environment – many of the emotional strains may linger and continue to cause difficulties.

Consider working with a therapist to unpick the experiences you have had. For me, this was really helpful and it also allowed me to see that some of the ways I was behaving and acting in my new school were adding to the stress and anxiety I was feeling. There will be triggers that take you back to previous challenges: if I am in a staff meeting now, for example, it still takes me some time to calm down – and that is more than five years later. The stigma surrounding medication for stress and anxiety is dissipating and it is so important that you make the decisions that are right for you in terms of supporting your mental health.

There is no time frame for recovering from workplace trauma and such feelings may linger for a long time. Remember, however, that the challenges you may have faced will give you a strength that you might not yet recognise. You will develop more compassion, more awareness of the fragility of life, and a deeper appreciation of the many schools that work brilliantly as collectives. Your experiences will also make you a better and more sensitive teacher. The more you have been through yourself, the more empathetic you will be to the needs of pupils, especially those who might be internalising their feelings.

Serene summary

Toxic school environments exist and it is vital that, as a profession, we recognise their characteristics – this will help us to limit their impact. If you are working in such an environment, make sure you prioritise your own health and wellbeing and maintain a healthy sense of perspective. Although no school is perfect, it is important to hold on to your professional values and leave an environment that is not suited to you.

PART IV: IN THE CLASSROOM

> 'Do not judge me by my success, judge
> me by how many times I fell down
> and got back up again'
> Nelson Mandela

18. THE BEHAVIOUR MENTALITY

Anxious anecdote

There are 10 minutes before Year 9 enter the room.

No, that's not quite right. There are 10 minutes before Year 9 become the room: before they pile in, laughing, shouting, pushing each other, continuing whatever frolics or arguments have dominated their lunch break.

That means there are 15 minutes to go before the teacher attempts the opening gambit that might gain the attention of a third of the class at best: "Right, I would like to start the lesson now."

The teacher will sit at the laptop and wait, hugely conscious of the physical symptoms of anxiety surging through his body. His stomach in knots, he will feel his breathing tightening. He will check his watch again, add another "engaging" image to the PowerPoint and run obsessively through the lesson content in his head.

Every teacher knows what the 10 minutes before the start of the lesson feel like. There are the nerves that begin to manifest in the stomach, the rapidly increasing heart rate. We recognise the futility of mentally rehearsing the lesson, yet we still play it out. Inevitably, James will have forgotten his ADHD medication and will be impossible to calm; Chloe will have (loudly) fallen out with Michaela. Yet again, the carefully curated lesson will fall apart.

The first and perhaps most obvious test for teacher resilience is challenging classroom behaviour. Conversations abound about behaviour management. I've lost count of the number of "top 10 strategies for managing poor behaviour" that I have read. I've had – and I'm sure I will continue to have – many conversations about behaviour that have served only to heighten my feelings of anxiety and make me feel deeply inadequate.

A few well-used but entirely useless phrases are casually thrown around. My personal "favourite" is the first, which is often combined with a exaggeratedly raised eyebrow:

- "Really? She is perfect for me."

- "Try to be more consistent."
- "Don't show any signs of weakness."
- "Don't smile before Christmas."
- "You need to make lessons more engaging."

These simplifications of a hugely complex craft overlook just how raw it feels to be faced with poor behaviour. Adrenaline will get us through the lesson itself, but what about the anxiety, self-loathing and internal battering that we will be left with after the lesson?

I'm not embarrassed to admit that the teacher in this chapter's Anxious Anecdote is me. It was my first year in a new school and I taught this Year 9 class for three 75-minute lessons a week, each falling in that dreaded after-lunch period.

In my previous role, as discussed earlier, I had been masquerading as a sharply dressed senior leader. I thought I had behaviour licked: after all, I was the teacher who had been entrusted with all-boy groups of inner-city London students. But stripped of this prestige, with no reputation, in a school that had just been placed in special measures, I was completely out of my depth. No longer could I get by on personality alone. I made the situation worse by hunkering down and not asking for help. I felt completely humiliated – I was supposed to be an experienced teacher who had come from the bright lights of management in London.

I would love to reveal here that I turned the class around and that by the end of the year they were kittens, happily lapping knowledge from my palm. They weren't: teaching doesn't always work like that. I didn't win them all over and much of the year felt like a battle. Since then, I have tried to learn from my mistakes, but I haven't always got it right.

Some teachers naturally find behaviour management easier, but no teacher has ever perfected behaviour in the classroom. For me, the experience of not getting it right with those challenging Year 9 students was important – it helped me to regain the humility that is integral to being effective in the classroom. This humility ensures that we never fall into the trap of taking the behaviour and engagement of young people for granted.

Behavioural anxiety

Anxiety about classroom behaviour can be a vicious circle that helps neither our capacity to manage behaviour, nor the way young people respond in our lessons. That anxiety comes with traps that are a recipe for disruption and unhappiness in the classroom:

1. **Catastrophising**. When we are anxious about the behaviour of a class, or individuals, we often expect the worst. We anticipate the lesson being derailed and predict how low we are going to feel afterwards. That puts us on edge before a lesson has even begun – those feelings are evident to the students, increasing the chance of things going awry.
2. **Negativity**. Our anxiety needs an outlet and this can means that we allow our negativity bias to go into overdrive. We are hyper-vigilant towards the students and berate them over the slightest infraction. Sometimes, shouting starts to dominate the room. But this friction serves only to increase the tension – young people fight negativity with more negativity.
3. **Losing perspective**. Anxiety can skew our thinking about the class and the individual students. Instead of recognising that some of them have engaged well with the content, we fixate on the young people who haven't – we perceive them as having spoiled the learning with their poor behaviour.

Once again, we need to think proactively about how we can prevent feelings of anxiety and stress from tarnishing our relationship with a class. The first thing we need to consider is what we can actually control.

Taking control

The possessive pronoun "my" can be hugely empowering for teachers. The young people enter into *our* classrooms – and that philosophy needs to run through everything that happens in them. A sense of powerlessness can arise from highly disruptive behaviour, but when we set the parameters and dictate how our classroom functions, we feel more of the calm and assertive control that young people need to see from us.

Let's consider seating arrangements: I can't think of any reason why a teacher would let young people sit where they want. This is never anything but an open invitation for inattentive and poor behaviour. But, rather than being rigid, the seating plan needs to be fluid, constantly changing and evolving. Those tweaks and refinements help us to find the right balance and get young people working in the way we want them to.

Then there's the application of rules and boundaries. I'm not a fan of co-constructing rules and classroom ways of functioning – I think teachers need to be in control. I appreciate that this is probably a manifestation of an anxious mind, but I'm comfortable with that. Outlining exactly what we expect, then being rigorous in demanding it, will mean that we are not taken advantage of. And, of course, sanctions need to be applied clearly and consistently. The hope is that once the students realise their behaviour has consequences, they will start to respond in ways conducive to a positive classroom atmosphere.

To allow for a moment of hyperbole, we can look to the words of Winston Churchill, a model of single-minded persistence and a man who could no doubt teach us a thing or two about resilience. Although I would be reluctant to describe students as "the enemy", the following quote speaks of the fact that a siege mentality is sometimes required in the classroom:

> *"Never give in – never, never, never, never, in nothing great or small, large or petty. Never give in except to convictions of honour and good sense. Never yield to force; never yield to the apparently overwhelming might of the enemy."*

Getting students onside

Making lessons interesting is a perpetual teacher challenge, but it is part of ensuring engagement and good behaviour among students. Interest can be elicited in many different ways: through our own persona and enthusiasm; through appealing content; through relationships; through additional resources.

What quickly becomes apparent is that young people's tolerance for gimmicks is low. Although there may be some initial novelty value, interest is quickly lost. But framing your subject in narratives, allowing students to exercise their intellectual curiosity, and offering regular and precise feedback will generate a genuine interest in your subject and help to maintain a positive atmosphere in the classroom. We have to work very, very hard to win some young people over – and sometimes it can take years. What we can never do, however, is give up on that noble aspiration. That means giving young people fresh starts and seeking to value and understand them as individuals – engaging with them on a human level.

Pre-lesson anxiety: visualisation

As quirky as it sounds, pre-lesson visualisation is something that I have found very helpful in dealing with challenging classes. I spoke to the psychologist Paul Gilbert, who has written a number of books on depression and anxiety, for my podcast[60] and he outlined how teachers can apply the techniques of visualisation. He suggested that we visualise ourselves in the way we want to appear – calm, composed and in charge – in order to combat feelings of uncertainty.

While this might sound a bit unnatural, the psychological premise is sound. Rather than our minds being flooded with negativity, we imagine ourselves in control – no matter what we are faced with.

---

60   tinyurl.com/y2talf3x

When we are experiencing pre-emptive anxiety, we start to exaggerate the difficulties and challenges we will face. In my battles with that Year 9 class, I would have visions of the class descending into complete uproar: chairs being thrown and abuse being hurled at me. Of course, things were never that bad. Asking ourselves, "What's the worst that might happen?" can help us to maintain a healthy perspective.

Anxiety and stress can, of course, manifest themselves physically. In my case, they usually add a degree of frantic energy to my communication. I know I need to take steps to appear assertive and in control. Slowing down my rate of speech has a positive impact, as does using my voice in ways that help to engage the room. Dropping and raising our voices can make our teacher talk more interesting and create more of that elusive quality, presence. We should also be conscious of using our body language in measured ways that communicate clarity and calm.

Cultivating compassion

It is always important to remember that young people experience all kinds of challenges outside our classrooms. Those challenges can mean that they interact with adults in a way that reveals resentment and a lack of trust. That is part of working with young people.

Remembering that we are the adult in the interaction and that the reasons for their behaviour are complex can help us to avoid taking things personally. These five simple steps can serve to cultivate the necessary compassion:

1. Smile and be warm.
2. Engage on an individual level.
3. Listen.
4. Model manners.
5. Give positive reinforcement – for example, phone calls or emails home.

Never give up on trying to build positive relationships. Being a bigger version of yourself and enforcing classroom routines will help.

Playing the long game

Behaviour management is relentless. In my training year, when I was taking an experienced teacher's class, that teacher described it as a "war of attrition". The following words from Margaret Thatcher (a resilient figure if ever there was one) could be written for a behaviour management training session: "You may have to fight a battle more than once to win it."

Perhaps the kindest thing we can do, in terms of our own capacity to manage stress and anxiety, is to always bear in mind the complexity of working with young people. The simple fact is that no matter how hard we try, there will always be things we cannot control. Expecting perfect behaviour from young people – and then berating ourselves when we fail to achieve it – will only make us more anxious and stressed.

Determination and resilience, however, are interlinked: never give up on those challenging classes and you will build a steely resilience that will last a lifetime.

Serene summary

Anxiety about behaviour management is entirely natural. Working to manage the things we actually have control over will help us to feel calmer and more able to be responsive to young people. Using support networks and being open about the reality of what happens in our classroom will also help to alleviate stress and anxiety.

19. PLANNING

Anxious anecdote

Sunday, midday. Caroline is planning for her week ahead. A PGCE student, she will be teaching six lessons across Monday and Tuesday (the first two days of her second placement).

This seems to her a fairly terrifying number. Luckily, her friend has passed on some inspiration about a detective lesson that explores the causes of deforestation. Caroline thinks it sounds really good: lots of group work and lots of the student-led learning that her new mentor seems so keen on.

Time to get designing. Each group needs a deforestation information sheet, a "forest of fun" support sheet and a "tree of confidence" rating.

Sunday, 6pm. One lesson finished, five to go.

The blank lesson plan makes it utterly explicit: we are the architects of our students' experiences. This is an exciting and creative opportunity, but it can lead to overthinking and feelings of stress. Questions abound: how exactly do we structure learning? And what tasks should we include?

The process of designing an effective lesson is complex and dependent on a number of variables. Early in our careers, lesson planning can keep us working into the small hours of the morning. Although, as a PGCE student, spending hours preparing a lesson is part of the excitement and process of learning how to teach, it is not manageable on a full timetable of more than 22 hours a week.

So, how can we make the process of lesson planning – and deciding what to teach – easier and more effective?

Simplify, simplify, simplify

If we are serious about teaching being a sustainable profession, then we need to be ruthless in simplifying what happens in our classrooms. Planning is an important part of that: it is the mechanism by which we edit our teaching, in an attempt to bring clarity and purpose to what happens in our classrooms.

Instead of packing our lessons full of resources and activities that merely fill time, we need to place *thinking* at the core of our planning. What exactly do we want young people to be thinking about and therefore learning? Focusing on this question will strip away all the additional "fluff" that can dominate modern teaching. We need to find clarity about the objective of the lesson.

Defining the objective

Lesson objectives come in many shapes and sizes, and there is debate about their efficacy in teaching and learning. In terms of streamlining and providing direction, however, they are important. The best lessons I have observed all had the same thing in common: a clear purpose that helps students to understand how what they are doing will aid their learning. In the next chapter we will explore why differentiating lesson objectives leads to reduced expectations. But a single overarching aim will help students to understand what they are doing and how they can do it successfully.

In terms of using lesson time effectively, it is important that the aim for the lesson is not just didactically presented to young people. Often, the objective is merely flashed up on a PowerPoint slide, then quickly forgotten about. Some kind of conceptual engagement is needed: young people need to be able to discuss the objective and identify exactly what it means. Writing it down in their books would be pointless – a mere act of copying that requires no intellectual engagement with the content.

Let's take an example of an overall objective in an English lesson:

"To evaluate how the poet Carol Ann Duffy presents love in *Valentine*."

There are key words in here that need to be discussed with students: "evaluate" is one that many will not be able to define and engage with. The focus on love will also need to be deconstructed, most likely with an initial conversation about the varying ways in which love is manifested. The objective needs to be returned to periodically throughout the lesson, as the class trace how close they are to engaging with this particular presentation of love.

We also need to give serious consideration to the effectiveness and efficiency of the resources we use alongside the lesson. There is one tool in particular that seems to have become married to the process of lesson planning: PowerPoint.

The PowerPoint prop

For many teachers, a lesson is incomplete unless it has a PowerPoint attached to it. The ubiquity of PowerPoint in the classroom is evident in the way young people's eyes drift apathetically towards the projector screen as they enter the classroom. That apathy is no doubt aided by the fact that almost every learning experience is coupled with a PowerPoint. Monotony and repetitiveness are the death of student engagement, so there is certainly a case for rethinking our reliance on PowerPoint.

I have been writing about PowerPoint and its efficacy in terms of time management and lesson content for some time. This is from a blog post I wrote in 2016, entitled "The curse of PowerPoint: time to teach naked".

"A confession: PowerPoint has become the clothing of my teaching. It is there, draped over every lesson, always present. It exists in different manifestations: sometimes it is an ostentatious outfit, a three-piece suit if you will, that is at the very heart of all the content. Sometimes it is a little more skimpy – the shorts and T-shirt variation. Maybe a few images to provoke thinking. But it is always there, a ubiquitous presence in my classroom.

Until this week. This week I went naked.

It felt uncomfortable to shed it at first: I was exposed, sweaty, nervous, tentative. I kept checking behind me, waiting for a prompt, a guide, a reassuring voice that would tell me what to do with my students next.

I searched in vain for a gigantic and friendly central point to direct students to when I felt their attention wavering. I yearned for something to ask students to copy as my energy levels sagged. Nothing.

Despite waking on Tuesday in a cold sweat, as the days went on, I started to feel more at ease in my nakedness: freer, looser, like a weight had been lifted from my shoulders. Bones of creativity creaked slowly and reluctantly into action. By the end of the week I was a full-on nudist, liberated in a manner I hadn't felt for years, removed from the shackles that had stolen so much of my time.

The curse of the PowerPoint has been lifted."

The analogy isn't my most subtle, but the point still stands: PowerPoint doesn't need to clothe our teaching. It is a fascinating and beneficial experiment to strip it away and assess the results in terms of managing our time and our students' learning.

Although it can be useful to start by challenging yourself to go a week without PowerPoint, this might not suit everyone. The most important thing is to maintain a reflective openness about its impact. Here are some questions to consider:

1. Is it absolutely essential to have a PowerPoint to go alongside this lesson?
2. How will a PowerPoint aid student engagement and thinking?
3. Is the time I spend creating this PowerPoint going to be worth it in terms of student learning?
4. What could I use instead of a PowerPoint?

This is not to say that PowerPoint doesn't have a part to play in the process of learning. One of the most exciting things about being a teacher, however, is the creative freedom and autonomy we have to get young people interested in learning. Taking risks and trying new things in our classrooms help to energise us as well as our students.

The remote learning that young people have experienced as a result of the Covid-19 lockdown has only added to my scepticism about technology. It has reinforced my belief that relationships are at the heart of teaching, and shown me just how much young people need that interaction from us to support their learning. A PowerPoint pales in comparison to the presence of an engaging and dynamic teacher. Our dispositions – and the passion we have for our subjects – are what get young people excited about learning. These require no additional preparation, or exciting image, whatsoever.

Photocopying

Another time-stealer in terms of lesson planning is the machine that so often appears to be deliberately mocking us first thing in the morning: it either refuses to do anything we ask of it, or it forces us to spend valuable minutes in a queue waiting to use its services. Too much of a teacher's time is spent getting wound up by the photocopier.

Preparing, photocopying and distributing resources in lessons can be time-consuming. And these photocopies are often just another thing to distract young people with – something quirky that might keep them busy for a few minutes. Then the inevitable "sticking sheets into their books" fiasco occurs, with sheets flying everywhere and a disastrous shortage of glue sticks.

We need to ask ourselves some hard questions about photocopying: does it add value in terms of helping young people to learn? Is it essential that a lesson has resources to go alongside it? Why do we need paper resources of this? And if I must photocopy this resource, can I reuse those photocopies at a later date? If I write a model answer, for example, I know I can use that resource many times and with different year groups.

If a lesson does require resources, the important thing is to be organised and plan in advance. Do everything possible to avoid adding to your morning anxiety by having to stand at a photocopier while you desperately watch the hands of the clock turn. Do your photocopying before you leave school at the end of the day or, even better, submit the resource to be copied in advance, if your school is lucky enough to have that service.

Content planning

Now we have streamlined our resources, we need to think about how we can apply this clear thinking to the lesson itself. Here is a five-point plan for saving time and improving the quality of lessons:

1. Have **clarity** about the objective. What exactly do you want young people to learn in the lesson, and what do you want them to do? This sounds very simple on paper, but it is the core of good planning. If we have clarity on the objective, we can design the learning around it.
2. How will we get the students **interested** and **engaged**? This is an important question for teachers and a simple truth: we need to work to make our content interesting and relevant for young people. Surprisingly, they might not all find the opening page of *Of Mice and Men* as riveting as I do. Sparking their interest might not require additional resources or preparation, just our own enthusiasm and passion. Or we could present something very simple, such as an image or object that relates to the topic and can get young people thinking about it. I don't believe in gimmicks or diluting learning in the classroom, but we have a responsibility to try to interest young people in what we are doing.
3. How are we going to **model** what we want them to achieve? Students need to see what the end product is supposed to look like and this can be presented in many ways. We might show them a previous student's attempt at the work, or we might go through examples together on the board.
4. What **questions** will help young people to understand the content? Our next chapter on differentiation will explore this in greater detail, but the types of questions we ask are vital in ensuring that the whole class develops conceptual understanding of a topic.
5. What **individual practice** will take place? We will only know whether our students have grasped the content once they have had the chance to produce something independently using what they have learned. This will likely take place in the later stages of a lesson and will require conditions that allow focus.

When planning lesson content, think about how you might reuse that content. Lesson episodes can be used many time, with different year groups

161

and different classes. Some tweaking will inevitably be required, but there is no shame in that, because it is better than constantly reinventing the wheel. Remember to keep your memory stick as organised as humanly possible: clear sections, clear weekly plans. And always back it up!

Long-term planning

My first school ingrained a number of bad habits in me. Because of the daily requirement to upload lesson plans to a shared system, I became a plan-on-the-day chap, arriving ridiculously early and writing streams for individual lesson plans. I had no idea how to plan for longer blocks of learning. This skill needs to be much more of a focus when it comes to supporting teachers. The more thoughtful and detailed a long-term plan is, the quicker and easier our daily planning becomes.

My half-term plan is now much more comprehensive, and I break this down into a weekly plan at the start of the week. This sense of control and direction not only gives the individual teacher confidence, but is also better for the learning of students.

Time planning

Planning should not be exclusive to lessons. It also pays to plan our time and to plan for pressure points over the week. I find lists are a very effective tool to aid this process.

Anyone with a serious interest in becoming more organised needs to read *The Organized Mind* by Daniel Levitin. He is another proponent of making notes and lists: "Writing things down conserves the mental energy expended in worrying that you might forget something and in trying not to forget it."

I have now fully embraced the list obsession that I spent so long scornfully mocking my wife for. Every morning, I make a prioritised list of how my time will be spent during the day and the order in which tasks will be completed. This is such an effective way to get rid of mental clutter and give direction to the day: my mind relaxes and is ready for action. Ticking off tasks is also very satisfying; any incomplete ones can be added to the next day's list.

There are so many time-stealers in teaching, and they can leave us overwhelmed and more likely to feel stressed. We need to constantly ask ourselves: what are the benefits of doing this? What would happen if I *didn't* do it? Do not be swayed by teachers who are always preparing "masterpiece" lessons that have young people swinging from the chandeliers and juggling thousands of resources. Keep things simple – and keep your sanity.

Serene summary

Place your lesson objective at the core of what you do – consider what you want your students to be thinking about. Resist the temptation to "fill" lessons with PowerPoints and resources. Instead, keep things calm and clear, allowing young people to focus on their learning.

20. DIFFERENTIATION

Anxious anecdote

"John, I would like you to complete this sheet. David, can you do this one, please?"

John glanced over at David's sheet: it was twice the length of his and without the large "helpful hints" section at the bottom of the page.

"Miss, why has David got more than me? Am I thick?"

The teacher replied: "No, John, I just think you will do better with this sheet."

John turned to David: "Good luck with that, mate, it's going to take you forever! I can just copy from this bit at the end of the page!"

Differentiation, and the multitude of ways that it can be interpreted, is the trigger for a great deal of teacher stress. And this stress often manifests itself in one emotion: guilt. We constantly question whether we are doing differentiation correctly, whether we should be doing it at all, and whether there is something else we should be doing to support our students better.

In *The researchED Guide to Education Myths*, Greg Ashman captures this nagging feeling perfectly:

> *"You can ignore the spectre in a noisy room at a busy time, but as a teacher, it is ever present, stalking you, gently tapping you on the shoulder. You dare not look around because the horrifying visage is too much to bear. 'I am already stretched as thin as linguine – perhaps even spaghetti,' you think. 'Where could I find the time to plan for yet more differentiation?'"*

For an observation lesson, differentiation is rolled out in its full glory, with a range of resources and worksheets to give the impression that this is our everyday practice. The reality, however, is completely different. It has to be, for the sake of our sanity.

The differentiation dilemma

In very simple terms, differentiation is about adapting and tailoring what we are doing to support the varying abilities in our classroom. But the definitions vary wildly when you discuss differentiation as a pedagogical tool with just a handful of teachers. Each has their own interpretation of what it means and how it functions in their particular classroom. As a profession, this is part of the challenge we face: how exactly should we be talking about differentiation, and what will have the most impact in terms of supporting students?

Lesson observation feedback can make the situation even more perplexing. Different observers will comment on different aspects of differentiation, and they might directly contradict advice that we have received before. The phrase "You need to differentiate more" is almost an automatic expectation at the end of a lesson observation – we never quite seem to get it right. Some observers still refer to one of education's most debunked myths: that we should cater to young people's "learning styles", despite the fact that research has pretty unequivocally demonstrated that learning styles do not exist.

There is no questioning the validity of the principle of differentiation: of course we need to tailor what we do to the individuals in our classroom. The trouble is, there is no definitive guidance to help us reflect on the different methods and approaches that will help each young person to achieve their potential. Instead, individual teachers have to decide what they consider to be best practice in different learning environments.

Context is also extremely important: how can we differentiate effectively when we have a full teaching timetable, with large classes of varying abilities, plus the conflicting pressures that exist for the modern teacher? In a paper entitled "Contested knowledge: a critical review of the concept of differentiation in teaching and learning", the teacher Sasha Taylor concludes:

> *"Class sizes, planning time, resources, increased teacher responsibilities and arrangement for collaboration with colleagues, must be taken into account for consistent application and effectiveness of differentiation."*[61]

This illustrates the utopian nature of some perceptions of differentiation. We need to consider all aspects of teaching carefully in order to ensure that we have the capacity to use this tool effectively.

---

61   https://tinyurl.com/yyhkeev7

The pitfalls of differentiation

As any classroom teacher knows, thinking about how to use differentiation in the classroom on a daily basis opens up a Pandora's box of worry: should we aim to meet every single individual's needs in every class? Should we prepare different resources? How do we know what level our students are capable of working at? Should we act as facilitators and place young people at the centre of what is happening in the classroom?

The answers to these questions can generate a significant workload burden for teachers. For one observation when I was a trainee, I wrote 30 different guidance sheets for the students to use to support their understanding of a task (it won't surprise you to know I was rather on the earnest side). By the time the lesson actually arrived, I was utterly exhausted. I spent most of the lesson trying to juggle the millions of bits of paper while the class rioted. Needless to say, the observer wasn't hugely impressed and instructed me to think more carefully about how I used differentiation.

Plenty of advice exists about the importance of giving young people a choice in the work they complete – for example, asking them to pick from three levels of challenge. I know exactly what level I would have gone for as a teenager: the easiest. "Offer at least two different tasks in everything you do" is very easy to tell teachers, but it is remarkably challenging to execute. In fact, I would argue that the amount of work this creates for teachers is not sustainable. Of course, now and then we might provide a choice of final tasks in order to boost student motivation, but it is just not practical to expect this on a day-to-day basis.

Differentiation can actually make work far too easy for students. Instead of providing a scaffold to support their learning, it builds the whole construct for them. The Anxious Anecdote at the start of this chapter offers an example of this: the worksheet given to John demands very little of him; he might have been capable of doing more, but instead he has been given an invitation to do less. And the fact that he has been given simplified work is made explicit to him, because his peer is completing a more challenging task. Over time, John's confidence and ability will be weakened – his self-identity will be reduced to "the student who is expected to do less work". Intellectual challenge and making mistakes are, of course, key to any learning process. Our students have to be permitted to grapple with what Professor Robert Bjork calls "desirable difficulties".

Doing differentiation well

So, how can we have a differentiated classroom *and* retain some semblance of work-life balance?

The most obvious way to differentiate is through our **interactions** with young people. To do this, we need to develop a detailed knowledge of our students' abilities. In classrooms where this understanding is present, differentiation is very apparent in the rich interactions that take place. It is much more productive to take the time to truly understand each young person's attitudes and barriers towards learning than to create four different versions of the same worksheet.

Seating plans are another route to effective differentiation. Considering carefully the abilities and dispositions of students, and their physical position in the room, will help us to facilitate their progress and learning. Over time, as we grow to understand our students, a seating plan becomes less of a behaviour management tool and more of a differentiation tool.

Questioning is one of our most effective teacher tools and, unless we are pre-preparing some particularly rich and challenging questions, it requires little preparation on our behalf. Its merits as a form of differentiation, however, are significant. In *Teach Like a Champion*, Doug Lemov argues: "Asking frequent, targeted, rigorous questions … is a powerful and much simpler tool for differentiating than breaking students into different instructional groups."

There are three key ways to maximise the potential of questioning in our classrooms:

1. **Leave more pauses**. Mary Budd Rowe was an American educator who conducted pioneering research on the idea of "wait time". She found: "If teachers can increase the average length of the pauses at both points, namely, after a question (wait time 1) and, even more important, after a student response (wait time 2) to 3 seconds or more, there are pronounced changes (usually regarded as improvements) in student use of language and logic."[62] Leaving this three-second pause is differentiation in itself, giving all students in the room the time to cognitively engage with the material.
2. **Ask "What do you understand?" instead of "Do you understand?"** This very simple change in our language reframes the question to check for understanding. It requires students to articulate what they have learned and allows us to check the clarity of their response.
3. **Seek clarifications and expansions**. Don't always accept the first answer: delve deeper and encourage students to come up with more. This challenges their thinking.

Scaffolding
The process of scaffolding a final task can, again, be very simple and not take up huge amounts of a teacher's time. High expectations are key: we must not overly

---

62   https://tinyurl.com/ya9xscrb

simplify the material and give students too much support. After all, they need to struggle and experience difficulties in order to learn and achieve.

The first step in scaffolding a challenging goal is to model it to the class. For my own subject, English, this might involve talking students through how I would approach a piece of writing. This provides an initial layer of support and begins to make your expectations clear. Modelling is itself an excellent way to differentiate, but time needs to be invested in exploring what might be right and why – and, indeed, what might be wrong.

Some kind of supportive framework can be given to students to aid their individual completion of the task. For example, a set of key reminders on a PowerPoint slide, prepared with the students so they are involved in the process.

It *is* possible to have a differentiation-rich classroom without giving up your evenings and weekends. Differentiation needs to become a clearer and more practical term. Once we have clarity on what differentiation should actually look like in practice, then we will be better able to find balance and resilience in our work.

In the next chapter, we will address the most time-consuming and pressurised form of differentiation: feedback. This can be a fraught aspect of the profession that tests the resolve of teachers and has resulted in thousands of wasted hours. Can we find a balance – one that keeps us from feeling overwhelmed but also helps to move forward young people's learning?

Serene summary

Beware the virtue signalling that exists with some forms of differentiation. Instead, think deeply about what will work for your students and what is sustainable for you. Cut back on preparation of resources and instead base your differentiation on scaffolds, modelling and the power of questioning.

21. FEEDBACK

Anxious anecdote

Alesha paused as she walked into the living room. Dalia was surrounded by her students' books; by her hand were three highlighter pens in different colours. Alesha watched as Dalia alternated expertly between the pens. The concentration on her face was something to behold.

"What are you doing?" Alesha enquired, genuinely perplexed.

Dalia snapped back to reality, holding her pink highlighter in mid-air. "Marking my books," she replied. She presumed the simplicity of her response would allow her to get straight back to work. She was rather proud of the rainbow-style feedback she gave her students and had beamed with pleasure when management had described her books as "a thing of beauty" in a staff training session last week.

"Why are there so many colours?" Alesha asked.

Dalia sighed. Then, with no hint of irony, she said: "Pink is for 'think', white is for 'not quite right' and yellow is for 'clever fellow'."

If we could gather together a thousand teachers and ask them the one thing that makes achieving work-life balance more of a challenge, we could be confident that marking would be right up there. Marking steals our evenings and our free time; it is the job that is never done.

Schools with ludicrous marking policies do not help staff in this regard – Dalia's colour-coded marking is not fictional. By asking teachers to adopt marking practices that are not supported by research evidence, the profession is reduced to one in which staff have no autonomy and are at the mercy of the whims of management.

Marking expectations differ vastly from school to school. There is little agreement on how much work should be marked and in what way. What one school might consider good marking would be considered poor practice in another. Our resilience is tested when we are overworked and overstretched, and marking is one of the main reasons why teachers struggle to manage their to-do lists. How, then, can we make marking easier to manage?

Feedback, not marking

Feedback is integral to any learning process. As Microsoft co-founder Bill Gates has said, "We all need people who will give us feedback. That's how we improve." As the experts in our classrooms, we have a responsibility to scaffold and support young people's learning. The mechanisms and manner in which we open up a dialogue with them about their work are very important.

Unfortunately, this "dialogue" has become very one-sided and often takes the form of excessive written comments in students' books. The culture of "workbook reviews" has added to the idea that ownership of student work has been transferred to teachers. Marking becomes something that is "performed" for an external audience, rather than something that aids young people in their learning and helps them to own and take pride in their work.

In my first book, *Slow Teaching*, I wrote at length about how detrimental this policy has been. So, the purpose of this chapter is only to present ways in which teachers can make feedback more manageable. And, of course, marking is just one type of feedback. There are all kinds of other ways in which we can open up a dialogue with students about their performance.

Feedwalks

Very often, as teachers, we waste precious time in our lessons. While my students are working individually, I am prone to aimless wandering around the room, offering generic praise here and there and commenting on how much time is left, breaking lots of concentration along the way. Instead, I could be using this time to offer specific, tailored feedback. I could use the time to talk to individual students in detail about their work, and have the conversations that are vital for building effective relationships. Sometimes, I might do this while brandishing a red pen and explaining the rationale for my comments.

Signalling the purpose of these "feedwalks" is important, so that students have clarity on what you're doing and why. That might sound something like this:

- "I'm going to be looking and marking for literacy while I walk around the room."
- "I'm going to correct at least two of your answers as I walk round the room."
- "I'm looking for the best pieces of work while I circulate."

After you've circulated, write up some whole-class feedback while the students are still working on the task. You could do this on a PowerPoint slide, highlighting the common misconceptions. This saves time and clears up misconceptions immediately.

Questioning is a brilliant tool for continuing the dialogue and making sure it is useful for students. Don't ask, "Do you understand my feedback?" Instead say, "Tell me what you understand from my feedback." This ensures that students have conceptualised your comments and can offer a rationale for why you have guided them in a particular way.

Visualisers

The visualiser has become a must-have tool for any teacher serious about preserving their work-life balance. As you know, I am a technological Luddite, so I was wary of visualisers for some time. But I've learned that they can have a real impact on students' work.

Visualisers can be used when students have completed a task, in order to scaffold a piece of self-assessment. Taking the strongest answer from a class and placing it on a visualiser can lead to a useful deconstruction of why the answer is successful and what the student has done effectively. Keeping the answer on the visualiser while the students complete their own corrections can be a powerful method of modelling.

Coded feedback

Giving concise and precise feedback in books is much more likely to elicit what we really need: engagement and improvement from students. Too much red pen can be demoralising for young people and can discourage them from engaging with the content of your comments.

Instead, come up with a set of class codes and ask young people to write in their own targets. This can save time and mean that young people better engage with the summative comments they have received.

Ownership

The narrative around books needs to be focused on the student: it is their book, their work and their responsibility. That means they need to develop the capacity to proofread and take ownership of what is in their books. Time needs to be allocated for this process in every lesson and every teacher's mantra should be, "Read over and check the work you have done before you hand it in."

We need to be firm and refuse to spend time marking work that is sloppy and rushed. It should be an expectation that students redo work that is not up to standard.

Respond, respond, respond

If you have slaved over a set of books for hours and sacrificed the latest episode of *The Great British Bake Off*, then students must be expected to spend time considering your feedback. If not, your time will not lead to any learning gains – ultimately, it will have been wasted.

We need to bear this in mind every time we write a comment. What will the student be able to do with the comment? How will it transfer into an action for them? It is best for students to consider their feedback in silence, so they are able to think carefully about what has been written.

Deciding *how* students will improve their work is a necessary consideration: will they write a response to your feedback? Redraft their work? Try a particular technique? Like everything, this needs careful planning and scaffolding.

Mindset

The comparative mindset often strikes when it comes to marking, particularly when a transparent and open culture is lacking around students' books. Feedback needs to be a part of what happens in our classrooms, but we also need to make sure that it doesn't eat up hours of time, regardless of what the teacher down the hall is doing.

Instead of slavishly marking each and every piece of work, we need to ask at every opportunity: what will be the benefit for my student if I mark this work? This is at the core of being a skilled and reflective practitioner, as is deep scepticism about streams of red pen merely for the sake of it.

Serene summary

Feedback-rich classrooms are very important to students' development. The time we invest in feedback must connect directly to student outcomes, so we need to employ a wide range of approaches and think deeply about the kind of marking we do – and how much.

22. PARENTS

Anxious anecdote

"Shannon's behaviour can be challenging at times." Donald had been circling around this point for a while – finding the obligatory positives had been a real stretch.

He could already feel that this parents' evening appointment was not going to end well. The subtext was that Shannon was a complete and utter nightmare and regularly sabotaged Donald's French lessons.

"What do you mean by 'challenging'?" asked Shannon's mother. There was scepticism on her face and a flash of anger that Donald recognised from Shannon's own reactions to being confronted in his classes.

"She can be rude and disruptive, and doesn't seem to be able to control her emotions," Donald replied. He had answered far too quickly and instantly wished he could retract the comment.

"How dare you call my daughter rude? Of course she can control her emotions – she isn't a child. None of her other teachers have any problems with her. She says your lessons are boring!"

Engaging with parents is an important aspect of working with young people. Although most parents are wonderfully supportive, some can cause a host of additional stresses and strains for teachers. We have to be at the top of our interpersonal game to deal with the difficult conversations that can occur.

When those interactions go wrong, they go spectacularly wrong and can turn both parent and child against us – a toxic situation that can be hard to resolve. When we get these interactions right, however, they can lead to a significant improvement in our relationship with the young person involved and in the way they engage with learning. Parents can be a powerful source of support.

Therefore, we need a parental communication toolkit to make sure that our interactions with parents empower us, rather than drain us.

No surprises

The very worst thing that can happen in a parental conversation is that the parent feels bemused and frustrated that they haven't been informed of issues earlier. Often, parents are completely unaware that their child has been anything but delightful in lessons. Rather predictably, young Jimmy hasn't in fact been running home and explaining that his behaviour in lessons has been outrageous.

We need to be proactive in identifying issues early and sharing them with parents. Most parents will appreciate an early phone call that can help to prevent any deterioration in behaviour. Such a phone call should be couched in the positive: "Jimmy has shown lots of potential but his attitude has started to slip…"

Even better is to pre-empt difficult conversations by getting in touch with a positive comment about a young person. Some parents are bombarded with negative feedback about their child, so a phone call from a teacher can elicit a comment like, "Oh no, what has Jimmy done now?"

Try changing the narrative. Highlighting what the student has been doing well will boost their confidence. You will also create a bank of goodwill with the parent, which will make it much easier to have a difficult conversation at a later date.

The positive phone call home can be a lovely habit to start with a class, creating a celebratory and positive atmosphere. Every week, choose one student per class to be the recipient of a phone call home (in my own lessons, I give this student the very cheesy title "Thom's Titan").

Sensitivity and compassion

Using email to have a tricky exchange with a parent can be hugely problematic: misconceptions can be created and they can then be hard to clear up. A much better option is a phone conversation, but the very best option is a face-to-face discussion. This allows for a nuanced interaction, and any complexities and frustrations can be cleared up quickly.

Of course, face-to-face meetings can be the more stress-inducing of options, but the investment of time and thinking will be beneficial in the long run. Here are some ways to ensure that these meetings lead to a positive outcome:

1. **Offer a warm welcome**. First impressions are important in any professional context, and parents are quick to make judgements of teachers that confirm or deny the way their child has talked about us at home. Offer the parent a warm but professional welcome, remember to smile and, if possible, shake hands. This will help the parent to relax. Then, no matter how the conversation plays out, we must maintain that professionalism and stay unfailingly polite.

2. **Listen**. Launching into an immediate tirade about Jimmy's terrible behaviour will put everyone's defences up, particularly the parents and Jimmy himself. Instead, establish a reciprocal dialogue and try to avoid the impression of casting judgement. An effective way of opening up a conversation is to ask how the young person is finding the lessons. Then, try to get to the root cause of their challenging behaviour.

3. **Provide evidence**. Ultimately, the conversation will have to involve an honest account of what has been happening in lessons. The more evidence you have to support your view of the student's challenging behaviour or lack of effort, the better. A powerful way to make your point can be to present examples in the young person's workbook; you can also refer to the work of a student of similar ability who is making more effort. Other colleagues can share their views on the student's behaviour in their lessons; pastoral staff can also provide support. Of course, all this needs to be discussed sensitively – you don't want to give the impression that you have a vendetta against the student.

4. **Set goals and targets**. A conversation that is entirely negative will not have the desired result. Setting proactive goals that highlight the importance of a change of attitude will instead pave the way for a more positive outcome. This might involve setting targets for the amount of work completed in a lesson, or a focus on behaviour.

5. **Follow up**. The process needs to be circular, for everyone involved. Young people can be very good at saying the right thing at the right time, but as soon as they are back with their peers, they can revert to habitual behaviours. Regularly following up with parents and the student, and checking how they are finding their targets, will give meaning to the outcomes of the meeting and ensure consistency.

The pushy parent

Some parents may prove more challenging than others. Some really want their child to be challenged academically and there is absolutely nothing wrong with that philosophy – if more parents thought in this way then our jobs would be much easier. Unfortunately, some parents take this to the extreme: they ask for more work, more information and, ultimately, more of our (very limited) time. Sometimes, they seem able to see only their child and their child's development.

The pushy, overbearing parent can be tricky to manage. It is important not to over-promise and to remind them that you have a class of 30 (or more) students to deal with. Seek support from management – remember that they deal with difficult parent interactions all the time.

Try to depersonalise the situation. It is not about you and your teaching: the parent, understandably, just wants the best for their child.

The excuser

Another tricky parent is the one who blames everyone but their child. Adopting a calm and emotionally detached persona will help you to keep conversations with this kind of parent from becoming frustrating. Remember the earlier points about keeping evidence of the young person's attitude and outcomes – you need to be very clear about exactly what is going wrong and the impact of this on the student's learning.

As always, be sure to avoid making comments that are personal and related to the child's disposition. Talking about active *choices* and the young person's agency in the situation takes the judgement out of the conversation: "Jimmy has chosen to behave in a disruptive way."

Sensitivity and interpersonal skills are vital when dealing with parents. Everyone is trying to do their best, so always remain compassionate and reserve judgement. Focus on resolution, looking for the best ideas to help the young person.

Serene summary

Parents can test our resolve and patience, but it is important that we are clear and compassionate in our discussions with them. Maintaining professionalism and emotional detachment, evidencing everything and following up with action points will help to make sure that interactions go well. Never forget to find the positives about the young person!

PART V: LEADERSHIP

> 'Change will not come if we wait for some other person or some other time. We are the ones we've been waiting for. We are the change that we seek'
> Barack Obama

23. A LETTER TO LEADERS

Anxious anecdote

The weekly "staff briefing" started at 8am on Tuesdays. Staff were very aware that this occasion was poorly named; in whispers, they referred to it as the "staff beasting".

"Marking is still not as detailed as we would like," the headteacher began. "Some departments are not using the three-colour coded system effectively. We are seeing far too much yellow for 'clever fellow', and not enough probing and challenging white for 'not quite right'."

Five minutes later, the headteacher moved on to another of her favourite subjects: lesson observations. "When Ofsted return – and I'm sure I don't need to remind you we are due a progress report soon – they will be looking for students who are engaged and partners in the learning process. I would like to send you back to your classrooms with that in mind: how are you ensuring that young people are part of the learning process?"

With that, the staff trudged out of the room, their minds bouncing from their unmarked pile of books to what on earth "young people are part of the learning process" meant.

Dear leaders,

I am writing to you in the spirit of openness and collaboration that should be the hallmark of our profession. I am full of admiration for the work you do, and the care, compassion and drive that most of you demonstrate in your work with staff and young people.

We all know, however, that burnout, disillusionment and stress levels are too high in our profession, and that teachers are vulnerable to anxiety and depression. I am not ascribing blame to you for this – we all face pressures, and we are all trying to do our very best.

Reducing anxiety and helping – not hindering – teachers to be as optimistic and resilient as possible has to be a priority for all of us. As leaders, the responsibility of facilitating conditions that enable optimism and resilience lies with you, more than with any other.

As someone who has taught in a wide range of schools and has experienced burnout and heightened levels of stress, I want to point out some easy wins that can help you to prevent your teachers from becoming overwhelmed. I do not share these in the spirit of judgement – most of them have been formulated after reflecting on my own mistakes.

Listen to your staff

I have met so many wonderful leaders who put listening at the core of what they do. A culture of listening means that mutually respectful relationships, based on both support and challenge, can be at the heart of the school. To prevent frustrations and anxieties from building up, the lines of communication need to be open.

In your school, are there different channels to allow teachers to express themselves? Do staff know about these? Do they feel they can share their reflections on work-life balance? And do they know their concerns will be listened to?

Listening is also about observing non-verbal indicators that staff stress levels are heightened. Are they running around frantically without any real sense of purpose? Are they spending hours at work or experiencing fractious relationships with colleagues?

Support us with behaviour issues

My own research and conversations with teachers have shown me that behaviour is often the greatest challenge to teacher resilience. It can not only stop us doing our jobs, but it can also stop us sleeping at night. Poor behaviour among students can be utterly relentless and destroy a teacher's self-esteem.

Here are some questions to inspire further reflection:

- Is your school culture non-judgemental and open about behavioural issues, so teachers feel they are trusted and supported?
- Is there a focus on modelling the behaviours and the kinds of relationships we all want to see in the classroom?
- Is there rigour and drive among leaders to deal with poor behaviour?

Be kind

I am not naive – I have worked as a leader in one of the highest performing state schools in the country. I recognise that leaders have to achieve outcomes and that your role is to drive forward attainment. But you can do that and be human. You can do that and build a culture of openness and transparency. You can do that and smile.

Leadership is such a privileged position. If you will allow me, I will give in to a moment of English-teacher sentimentality and share these words from Wordsworth: "The best portion of a good man's life are his little, nameless, unremembered acts of kindness and love." People want to work for kind and supportive leaders, and they remember when they are treated well.

As a leader, you are being watched all the time and you cast all kinds of shadows. Do your actions match your words? Are you an energiser who allows people to learn and grow? Or do you always find fault and drain other people's confidence? The importance of kindness cannot be exaggerated in helping staff to be resilient and positive about their work. Such an ethos shows that conversations about teacher wellbeing are not tokenistic, but that they matter deeply to those who have responsibility to lead.

Prioritise work-life balance

If schools want to be full of teachers who are emotionally robust and have the energy required to teach effectively, then work-life balance needs to be a priority. It needs to be at the root of all conversations in school: how can we be the most effective and efficient with our time, and what are our boundaries?

Teachers are naturally diligent and can be their own worst enemies. Please don't burden them with excessive accountability regimes, pointless learning walks and endless workbook reviews. Open up discussions about ways in which staff can switch off and go home – and model this yourself. Don't treat staff like hamsters on a wheel who are there merely to churn out exam results.

Trust and empower your staff and we will rise to the challenge. It is why we went into teaching in the first place.

Be strategic

We need direction and clarity about what exactly is expected from us – and at what points in the year. You have more time available than the classroom teacher, so it is up to you to be as organised and proactive as possible, and to communicate openly with classroom teachers.

Knowing what is coming up allows us to emotionally prepare for busier periods and plan our time more effectively. Please don't use Ofsted, or other inspection agencies, as the metaphorical carrot or as a stick to beat us with. Instead, create a collective sense of what really matters: doing our very best for young people.

Empower teachers

In order for teachers to really develop resilience, they need to be empowered and trusted. If you give us an opportunity to exercise our leadership experience, then we will thrive, but this opportunity needs to allow us to genuinely make a difference in school, not just add to our workload. We all need to feel like we are growing and developing in our professional roles, so by considering the mechanisms by which we can achieve that, you will help us to move forward positively and become better teachers.

Schools need to be full of diverse individuals: we need the vitality and energy of new teachers, and the wisdom and experience of those who have honed their craft over many years. Nurturing teachers' resilience will help more to stay in the profession long-term. Young people will be the beneficiaries of their experience.

Yours sincerely,
Jamie Thom

24. LEADERSHIP CASE STUDIES: SUPPORTING TEACHER RESILIENCE

In this chapter, Stephen Ramsbottom and Jill Berry write about how leaders build resilience in their staff – and build their own resilience. How do leaders support staff to develop professionally and cope with the demands of teaching?

Stephen Ramsbottom, director of professional development at St Albans High School for Girls in Hertfordshire

In recent years, St Albans High School for Girls has been shifting its performance management process towards a more developmental process of professional reflection. In *Putting Staff First: a blueprint for revitalising our schools,* John Tomsett states: "I have never worked with a teacher who hasn't wanted to do a good job." Acknowledging this, and starting from a position of trust, our approach is driven by supported self-reflection in an atmosphere of continuous improvement, which seeks to nurture talent, ambition and career development.

Central to the process of professional reflection is the development of a coaching culture which emphasises the importance of:

- Listening with compassion and sincerity.
- Questioning skilfully to clarify and deepen thinking.
- Promoting clarity concerning the chosen actions.
- Providing appropriate support and challenge at the right moment.

Coaching for professional reflection

Although every member of the teaching staff receives coaching training, there are 20 highly trained volunteer super-coaches in the school, who coach all teaching staff. There are a minimum of three formal coaching sessions and any number of shorter, less formal conversations across a cycle (which we switched to two years to allow time for deeper thinking and meaningful engagement). The allocation of coach to coachees is done in a non-hierarchical, subject-neutral way. Where expert mentoring or focused instructional coaching is necessary, this is provided via the line management or peer-mentoring structures.

While there will always be some resistance to any significant change, the general response has been overwhelmingly positive. The evaluation of the first cycle included these comments, which highlight the supportive and developmental nature of coaching, contributing to staff wellbeing:

- **Aspirational**: *"The process gave me room to set ambitious targets without fear of failure."*
- **Developmental**: *"The coaching conversations crystallised my thinking and made me more aware of where I am now and what I need to do next."*
- **Individualised**: *"I felt more valued as a member of staff than I perhaps ever have done before."*
- **Empowering**: *"It encouraged me to consider myself as a person rather than 'just' the function that I needed to fulfil my different roles."*

A day for professional reflection

Meaningful professional reflection takes time, and this is why we now take one of the allocated Inset days and protect it for professional reflection. A dedicated day to pause, listen, question, think – and have the kind of deep, big-picture conversations that are difficult in a normal school day. The day is not an end in itself, but a visceral, explicit manifestation, indeed, a celebration of the road we are on – a cultural shift in the way we approach professional development.

The professional reflection day has three strands: professional reflection; community; and health and wellbeing. Within these strands is a wide menu of options, so each member of staff can select their own personalised tapestry of reflective activities.

Professional reflection: Typically, the professional reflection day is framed by a keynote speaker offering insight, inspiration and strategic stimulus. In 2019, Tom Sherrington led three sessions that synchronised with our regular professional development foci: "Teachers can only improve themselves, but how?", "The art of middle leadership" and "What I wish I had known when I started".

This final session was an open invitation to all local schools and ITT providers. In addition, time is allotted for coaching conversations, teaching and learning forums, mentoring sessions and departmental discussion. Staff are encouraged not to spend time on this day engaging with routine tasks such as planning, marking or photocopying.

Community: The activities and structure of the professional reflection day aim to provide the opportunity for staff to meet and talk, outside of normal departmental bubbles, fuelled by fine food and quality coffee. The centrepiece of this is an extended sit-down lunch and staff colloquium, where a number of staff share their passions, which may or may not be connected to their subject specialism. The goal of the staff colloquium is to celebrate the expertise and love of learning that exists within our teaching community and to help this to find outward expression more freely. Recent topics have included "How to appreciate a Mahler symphony" by a maths teacher, "The power of language" by an MFL teacher, "Deep-ocean volcanoes" by the headmistress, and "The art of seduction? An aria from Mozart's *Don Giovanni*" by an English specialist.

Health and wellbeing: Clearly, the health and wellbeing of staff cannot be addressed in a single day. At best, this would be tokenistic; at worst, patronising and insulting. Tackling staff health and wellbeing is not a box to be ticked but a culture to be developed and lived. However, running a wellbeing strand through the day does serve a number of purposes, providing:

- Space to reflect and process the input from the other sessions, in the same way that we often have our best thoughts in the shower or walking the dog.
- A forum where staff can openly discuss wellbeing issues.
- A platform for promoting the opportunities that exist for staff on a regular basis.

In recent years, the health and wellbeing strand has included a staff jog, an end-of-day staff walk (followed by a reflective beverage), yoga, swimming, badminton and talks from visiting speakers on topics such as self-awareness and emotional intelligence.

Professional development book club

The professional development book club meets once a fortnight for a relaxed but focused 45-minute discussion before school. Over the past few years we have read a wide range of books and articles, with different members of the group leading the discussion according to their particular interests. We have found that finding an appropriate pace of reading is very important, to balance the work/reading load against the need for momentum. Likewise, the timing of what we read is critical: *What If Everything You Knew About Education Was Wrong?* by David Didau was a great autumn-term study, as we started to review our teaching and learning strategy. Reading *Cleverlands* by Lucy Crehan was timed to coincide with the publication of the 2018 PISA results. *MARGE* by Arthur Shimamura was a low-input, high-impact read during a busy report-writing season. *A Quiet Education* by Jamie Thom prompted some deep reflection during the relative isolation of lockdown, followed by some thought-provoking Zoom discussions.

This regular, low-friction form of professional development contributes to staff wellbeing by:

- **Regularly reconnecting teachers with the bigger educational picture**. It is very easy to lose sight of the glorious ideals of education and for our vision to be clouded by the busyness and mundane minutiae of school life. Meeting with metronomic regularity to be challenged and stimulated by the best minds in education is refreshing and uplifting. It is a reminder of why we got into teaching in the first place. Many things are discussed at book club, but the key underpinning questions are always "What does this look like in our context?" and "What does this look like in my classroom?" Thus, there is a direct and powerful connection between the best educational thinking and daily practice.
- **Providing bottom-up professional development**. A group of education enthusiasts, passionate about teaching and learning, are keen to find out more and to get better at what they do. The resistance and cynicism that can accompany top-down approaches is absent; the discussions are positive, supportive and developmental.
- **Offering unforced, non-hierarchical, inter-departmental collaboration**. Thus, strengthening the common goal and purpose.
- **Combining intrinsic and extrinsic motivation**. Colleagues participate in book club because it is an enjoyable thing to do in its own right, satisfying our basic need for autonomy, competence and relatedness. But, over time, the book club has become increasingly influential, providing a form of extrinsic reward. For example, our reading has inspired and informed inquiry questions and secondments to SMT/SLT. Recently, the Year 7-11 tutor programme has been completely reimagined as a result of reading *MARGE* by Arthur Shimamura.

Workload and wellbeing

Fuelled by external attempts to raise standards, the past few decades have seen the growth of a toxic audit culture of performativity, characterised by graded lesson observations, hierarchical performance management systems and, in some cases, performance-related pay. The result has been well documented: unsustainable workloads and a disillusioned workforce. As Tom Sherrington wrote in 2017, "It seems blindingly obvious that our system of very high stakes inspection and performance measures has gone way past the point of having a positive impact".[63]

---

63 https://teacherhead.com/2017/12/13/accountability-stick-is-taking-us-to-the-brink-time-for-radical-change

The toxicity of this culture cannot be denied. The retention and recruitment figures do not lie. However, it is important, as a result, not to oversimplify the relationship between workload and teacher stress and anxiety. The link between teacher workload and anxiety is not always a straight line.

Across almost 25 years of teaching and various leadership roles, my personal sense of wellbeing has been linked to job fulfilment, not workload. When there has been quality leadership with a clear vision, a sense of purpose with a healthy balance of support, and challenge, trust and the associated autonomy, my workload has increased but it has been enjoyable and purposeful. At other times and in different schools, I have found that weak leadership, unclear goals and a sense of drift – the feeling that nobody cares or would notice if you were doing a good or bad job – lead to frustration and disillusionment. This creates its own stress, even though the workload is reduced.

Jill Berry, leadership consultant and former headteacher

I had seven different jobs across a 30-year career in schools. I enjoyed my headship – during the last 10 years most of all. However, headship required reserves of resilience beyond anything I had ever experienced.

There were challenging times and difficult decisions – including staffing issues, child protection and safeguarding, and financial pressures – and I worked harder than I ever had before. Managing the pace and finding a sustainable balance in my life were key. It was crucial to ensure that I had clarity of purpose, and strong values and principles that underpinned the decisions I was called upon to make when we faced the most demanding situations.

Looking back, I see how my resilience grew over time. I would describe myself as sensitive: I do feel things deeply and I will always maintain that this is a strength, not a weakness. Leaders need empathy and the capacity to recognise how others feel, too. But they also need the ability to move past this and do what needs to be done without being derailed by the strongest emotions. I often think there's a similarity with the role of a medical professional. If you don't care about your patients, you will be a poor doctor. But if you care too much about your patients, you will be a poor doctor. A degree of objectivity, and the recognition that we are rational as well as emotional beings, do help with respect to resilience.

I knew I was becoming more resilient as my experience grew and I gained confidence. I recognised this was happening because my capacity to feel something, then recover and move on, speeded up. I would walk into school and reflect that the previous day something had been very much on my mind. But on this morning, I felt better about it – I had recognised and experienced the emotion, processed it and moved beyond it, giving me the emotional space to meet whatever this day would bring. When I met challenges I had never faced before, I found it reassuring to remember that I had met new challenges before and survived them. I had found a way through. I knew that those who worked closely with me and knew me best – including my senior team and my governing body – had faith in my ability to do whatever needed to be done, and to step up, rather than step aside. All of this contributed to my developing resilience over time.

Sometimes I meet aspiring leaders who doubt that they have the resilience the role will require. I want to say to them: resilience isn't fixed. It can grow and strengthen, with experience and growing confidence. To a certain extent, we all learn how to do a job from doing the job – we build the bridge as we walk on it, to use Robert Quinn's words.[64]

Don't underestimate what you may be capable of.

---

64   Quinn, RE. (2004) *Building the Bridge As You Walk On It: a guide for leading change*, Jossey-Bass

CONCLUSION

> *God grant me the serenity*
> *To accept the things I cannot change;*
> *Courage to change the things I can;*
> *And wisdom to know the difference*

Every day in a school environment, a teacher's resilience is tested in a multitude of ways. Often, that test is invisible, so we don't always appreciate at the time just how much mental strain we are experiencing. Making those implicit moments explicit, in the writing of this book, has filled me with even more admiration and respect for the work that teachers do day in, day out.

Our profession is a demanding one that requires courage and fortitude, but it is also one that is transformative and profoundly important. I hope that by reading this book, you have found some solace and comfort in knowing that we all struggle to some degree with stress and anxiety. I also hope that these pages might prove helpful in fostering a resilient mindset that allows you to achieve longevity in the profession.

Young people depend on us to stay resilient – to look after our own physical and mental wellbeing – so that we can provide them with the best education we possibly can. That is our core purpose and it should encourage us to make our wellbeing a priority. We need to build an outlook that is positive and optimistic.

Establishing new habits and sticking to positive changes can be challenging, but it is also an empowering process. The effort and discipline required remind us, to paraphrase the final lines of William Ernest Henley's poem *Invictus*, that we are the masters of our fates and the captains of our souls. This poem, which inspired Nelson Mandela and whose title translates as "unconquerable", can fuel us in our own modest attempts to help our young charges.

When I teach that poem, which is at every opportunity, I finish the lesson by asking the young people to stand and speak those learned lines in unison, with fists raised. At first their performance is whispered and tentative, but the volume grows as they lose the self-consciousness, until with encouragement they are shouting the words as loud as they can.

It is an image and a philosophy that I would like to conclude with, except here it is we teachers, not our students, who need to remember the message. Teachers need to know that the work they do is profoundly important and that they are ultimately in charge of their own capacity to thrive in this profession. That knowledge, I hope, can support the development of true inner resilience.

ACKNOWLEDGEMENTS

As always, I would like to thank my wife, Fiona, for her love, support and understanding. Her inner resilience is remarkable and I learn every day from her capacity to cope. Our wee boy, Christopher (now officially potty-trained), also deserves a thank you. I will always remember and cherish our lockdown months as a family.

Thank you to my mum and dad for their support and encouragement, and for the constant educational inspiration.

Thank you to all at John Catt, particularly Alex Sharratt and Jonathan Barnes, for the opportunity to write another book and the unwavering support. I am so grateful for the faith you have in my ramblings. Thank you to Isla McMillan, for understanding the purpose of this book and your care and attention to detail in improving it. Again, this book is so much richer and better for all your hard work on it. I promise I will not subject you to another of my books for a long time – two in one year is more than enough!

Thank you to all the teachers who read drafts of this book, offered encouragement and got in touch about their own experiences. I am profoundly grateful and *Teacher Resilience* is richer for the feedback.

Thank you to all those in education who have contributed to the book and supported it. A particular thank you to Kat Howard, for such a generous and thoughtful foreword, and Jill Berry and Stephen Ramsbottom for their brilliant and helpful leadership case studies.

REFERENCES

Ashman, G. (2019) "The differentiation myth" in Barton, C (ed), *The researchED Guide to Education Myths*, John Catt

Atwal, K. (2019) *The Thinking School: developing a dynamic learning community*, John Catt

Avalos-Bevan, B and Bascopé, M. (2017) "Teacher informal collaboration for professional improvement: beliefs, contexts, and experience", *Education Research International*

Buck, A. (2020) *The BASIC Coaching Method*, Cadogan Press

Crehan, L. (2016) *Cleverlands: the secrets behind the success of the world's education superpowers*, Unbound

Curtis, C. (2019) *How to Teach English: novels, non-fiction and their artful navigation*, Independent Thinking Press

Didau, D. (2015) *What If Everything You Knew About Education Was Wrong?*, Crown House Publishing

Frank, A. (2012) *The Diary of a Young Girl: the definitive edition*, Penguin

Gilbert, P. (2017) "Compassion: definitions and controversies" in Gilbert, P (ed), *Compassion: concepts, research and applications*, Routledge, pp.3-15

Goleman, D. (1996) *Emotional Intelligence: why it can matter more than IQ*, Bloomsbury

Goleman, D. (2007) *Social Intelligence: the new science of human relationships*, Arrow

Goleman, D and Davidson, R. (2017) *The Science of Meditation: how to change your brain, mind and body*, Penguin

Goodley, C. (2018) "Reflecting on being an effective teacher in an age of measurement", *Reflective Practice* 19 (2) pp.167-178

Goodwin, DK. (2009) *Team of Rivals: the political genius of Abraham Lincoln*, Penguin

Gros, F. (2014) *A Philosophy of Walking*, Verso Books

Hargreaves, A. (1995) "Beyond collaboration: critical teacher development in the postmodern age" in Smyth, J (ed), *Critical Discourses on Teacher Development*, Cassell, pp.149-179

Hari, J. (2018) *Lost Connections: uncovering the real causes of depression – and the unexpected solutions*, Bloomsbury

Harris, D. (2014) *10% Happier*, Yellow Kite

Hayes, MC. (2018) *Write Yourself Happy: the art of positive journalling*, Octopus Publishing Group

Jay, M. (2018) *Supernormal: childhood adversity and the untold story of resilience*, Canongate

Korb, A. (2015) *The Upward Spiral: using neuroscience to reverse the course of depression, one small change at a time*, New Harbinger

Lemov, D. (2010) *Teach Like a Champion*, Jossey-Bass

Levitin, D. (2015) *The Organized Mind: thinking straight in the age of information overload*, Penguin

Mandela, N. (1995) *Long Walk to Freedom*, Abacus

McEwen, BS, Gray, JD and Nasca, C. (2015) "Recognizing resilience: learning from the effects of stress on the brain", *Neurobiology of Stress*, vol. 1, pp.1-11

Murakami, H. (2003) *Norwegian Wood*, Vintage

Myatt, M. (2016) *High Challenge, Low Threat: finding the balance*, John Catt

Neff, KD. (2009) "The role of self-compassion in development: a healthier way to relate to oneself", *Human Development* 52 (4) pp.211–214

Newport, C. (2019) *Digital Minimalism: choosing a focused life in a noisy world*, Portfolio

Nhat Hanh, T and Weare, K. (2017) *Happy Teachers Change the World: a guide for cultivating mindfulness in education*, Parallax Press

Ricard, M. (2018) *Altruism: the science and psychology of kindness*, Atlantic Books

Robertson, B. (2020) *The Teaching Delusion*, John Catt

Sacks, O. (2015) *Gratitude*, Picador

Sacks, O. (2015) *On the Move: a life*, Picador

Sarason, SB, Davidson, KS, Lighthall, FF, Waite, RR and Ruebush, BK. (1960) *Anxiety in Elementary School Children*, Wiley

Scott, K. (2017) *Radical Candor: be a kick-ass boss without losing your humanity*, St Martin's Press

Shimamura, A. (2018) *MARGE: a whole-brain learning approach for students and teachers*, CreateSpace

Shulman, LS. (2004) *The Wisdom of Practice: essays on teaching, learning, and learning to teach*, Jossey-Bass

Taylor, S. (2017) "Contested knowledge: a critical review of the concept of differentiation in teaching and learning", *Warwick Journal of Education* 1

Tomsett, J and Uttley, J. (2020) *Putting Staff First: a blueprint for revitalising our schools*, John Catt

Walker, M. (2017) *Why We Sleep: the new science of sleep and dreams*, Allen Lane